The Gold and the Dross

Brill Guides to Scholarship in Education

Series Editors

William M. Reynolds (*Georgia Southern University, USA*)
Brad Porfilio (*Seattle University, USA*)

Editorial Board

Donna Alvermann (*University of Georgia, USA*)
Antonia Darder (*Loyola Marymount University, USA*)
Petar Jandrić (*Tehničko veleučilište u Zagrebu, Croatia*)
Lagarrett J. King (*University of Missouri, USA*)
Sherell McArthur (*University of Georgia, USA*)
William F. Pinar (*University of British Columbia, Canada*)
Pauline Sameshima (*Lakehead University, Canada*)
Christine Sleeter (*California State University Monterey Bay, USA*)

VOLUME 1

The titles published in this series are listed at *brill.com/bgse*

The Gold and the Dross

Althusser for Educators

By

David I. Backer

BRILL
SENSE

LEIDEN | BOSTON

All chapters in this book have undergone peer review.

The Library of Congress Cataloging-in-Publication Data is available online at http://catalog.loc.gov

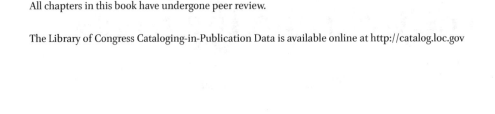

Typeface for the Latin, Greek, and Cyrillic scripts: "Brill". See and download: brill.com/brill-typeface.

ISSN 2590-1958
ISBN 978-90-04-39468-1 (paperback)
ISBN 978-90-04-39125-3 (hardback)
ISBN 978-90-04-39469-8 (e-book)

Copyright 2019 by Koninklijke Brill NV, Leiden, The Netherlands.
Koninklijke Brill NV incorporates the imprints Brill, Brill Hes & De Graaf, Brill Nijhoff, Brill Rodopi, Brill Sense, Hotei Publishing, mentis Verlag, Verlag Ferdinand Schöningh and Wilhelm Fink Verlag.
All rights reserved. No part of this publication may be reproduced, translated, stored in a retrieval system, or transmitted in any form or by any means, electronic, mechanical, photocopying, recording or otherwise, without prior written permission from the publisher.
Authorization to photocopy items for internal or personal use is granted by Koninklijke Brill NV provided that the appropriate fees are paid directly to The Copyright Clearance Center, 222 Rosewood Drive, Suite 910, Danvers, MA 01923, USA. Fees are subject to change.

Brill has made all reasonable efforts to trace all rights holders to any copyrighted material used in this work. In cases where these efforts have not been successful the publisher welcomes communications from copyright holders, so that the appropriate acknowledgements can be made in future editions, and to settle other permission matters.

This book is printed on acid-free paper and produced in a sustainable manner.

To Shelly, who had me at "Spinoza"

To know is not to extract from the impurities and diversity of the real and pure essence contained in the real, as gold is extracted from the dross of sand and dirt in which it is contained. To know is to *produce*...
    LOUIS ALTHUSSER, *Philosophy and the Spontaneous Philosophy of the Scientists and Other Essays: Theory, Theoretical Practice and Theoretical Formation: Ideology and Ideological Struggle*, 1990c, p. 15

Yet this is how philosophy proceeds. One word is enough to open up the space for a question, for a question that has not been posed. The new word throws the old words into disorder and creates a space for the new question. The new question calls into question the old answers, and the old questions lurking behind them. A new view of things is thus attained.
    LOUIS ALTHUSSER, *Philosophy and the Spontaneous Philosophy of the Scientists and Other Essays: Philosophy and the Spontaneous Philosophy of the Scientists*, 1990b, p. 87

Contents

Acknowledgements XI

Introduction XII
General Plan and Purpose of This Book XII
Althusser's Context XIII
Althusser's Life XV
Author's Context XVI
Note on Passages XVII

1 **A Beginner's Guide to Interpellation** 1
Getting in Trouble 1
At School 2
Get with the Program 3
Not Anything Impactful 4
I Don't Remember What I Learned in School 4
Testing 5
Where Did My Friends Go? 6
Falling in Love 8
Is Interpellation Passive? 9
Ideology = Imagined Relations to Real Conditions 10
Wings 10
Race and Gender 10
Reproduction 11
Consent 11
Individuality 11
Images 12
Being Guided 13
Interpellation Machine 13
Intersectionality 15
Counter-Interpellation 15
A Grain of Sand 16
Hut 17
A Play 17
Our Society: Capitalism and Democracy 18

2 **The Law of Dislocation** 20
Concrete-Real vs. Concrete-in-Thought 20

Snakes, Ropes, and Concepts   23
The Gold and the Dross   25
Straying from Dislocation: Empiricism and Surplus Value   27
Petty, Laplace, and Capital Vol. 1   29
Leaves, Monads, and Other Simple Internal Essences   30
Shades of Hegel   31
Expressivism: (Dig Here)   32
Human Nature   33
Concepts behind 'Words'   35
A Theory of Reading: Listening to Silence   36

3 **The Law of Uneven Development**   37
Every Thing Is a Mess   37
The DSA   40
Theory of Combination   41
Theory of Formation   42
Theory of Relative Autonomy   42
Theory of Determination   43
The Wrong Side of History   44
Acorns   46
Teleology on the Train   46
Concepts of Structure: Captain Planet vs. Voltron   48
The Two Laws: Three Reflections   50

4 **Theory of Social Formations**   53
Geology as Analogy for Society   53
Forces, Elements, and Variations in Society: Overview   54
Economic Region   55
Ideological Region   56
Culture and Agency   57
Repressive Region   57
Thanksgiving   58
The Three Social Forces: Productive, Reproductive, Repressive   60
The Hut and the Theater   60
Naked Capitalism   62
Home Ownership   62
Freedom   64
An Allegory for Social Structure   65
In the Last Instance: Theory of Movable Types   67

5 **Conclusion: Ideology, Truth, Science** 71
   Ambivalence 71
   Truth as Correctness 73
   Gold 75
   Science as Sweet Science 76

Afterword: Studying the Dross 78
   Tyson E. Lewis

References 81
Index 82

Acknowledgements

Thanks to Megan Laverty, Tyson E. Lewis, Derek R. Ford, Robbie McClintock, Jessica Lussier, Curry Malott, Awad Ibrahim, Warren Montag, Dave Mesing, Asad Haider, and Kate Cairns for invaluable guidance and friendship. Thanks to Brad Porfilio and Bill Reynolds for their invitation to write this book. And a very special thanks to Shelly Ronen for her partnership and tolerance of ontological questions.

Introduction

General Plan and Purpose of This Book

Louis Pierre Althusser was a French philosopher and educator. He was born in 1918 and died in 1990. He studied the German political economist Karl Marx, as well as commentators and politicians who had taken up Marx's thinking, to produce a Marxist theory.

Althusser did this because he thought that some of the people who had taken Marx's ideas the furthest were wrong. He disagreed with party orthodoxy. He was a devout member of the French Communist Party, refusing to leave it even when his students took to the streets of Paris in 1968 (he told them not to) and a New Left emerged, a Left that rejected the party form as a strategy for ending capitalism. Though he stayed in his party, he had actually been betraying it in an important way during his time as a member. Althusser's reading of Marxist philosophy was basically that most Marxists were not Marxists, and that the party had it all wrong. This philosophy would open new possibilities for understanding society and politics and education from a socialist and communist perspective—one that makes good sense now that the New Left is old.

Althusser famously said that no reading is innocent. This one isn't either. My reading of Althusser is a particular kind of educational reading for those who have never encountered Althusser's thought before, or perhaps even any kind of philosophy before. While abstract, I have tried to make sure the writing isn't too technical. While theoretical, I have tried to make it engaging as well. (I'm currently at work on a longer, more technical manuscript on Althusser's influence on educational thinking, due to be published in 2020.) This educational reading is therefore also an activist reading. It will, I hope, be useful for thinking deeply about how to unlearn capitalism and learn socialism. I therefore intend it for educators in the expansive sense of that term: organizers that teach; teachers that organize; campaigners that study; students that campaign.

The plan for the book: First, there's "A Beginner's Guide to Interpellation," which I first wrote as a pamphlet to help teachers understand Althusser's flagship concept of ideological reproduction. The pamphlet also serves as an introduction to basic terms in Althusserian theory: relations of production, repression, the subject, etc. After this introductory pamphlet, I elaborate two "laws" of Althusserian theory: the law of dislocation and the law of uneven development. These laws aren't hard and fast dicta, but rather theses that help organize/summarize basic facets of Althusser's thinking. Next comes a chapter on what the laws tell us about society and social change, or a theory of social formations, and finally a conclusion focusing on ideology and science.

Althusser's Context

But before the arguments, some background. Althusser's historical moment is crucial for understanding his philosophy. Althusser's persona and personal history are equally important to know.

Defined by membership in communist parties, people desiring an end to capitalism took their lead from Russia, whose communists came to power in an electrifying pair of revolutions in 1917. The fledgling communist state implemented some of the most progressive policies seen in a large nation and held onto that power through wars on multiple fronts. Communists in Russia brought Marx's ideas to life at a massive scale and capitalists the world over were afraid. Championing worker councils called soviets, Russian communists took state power for the first time in history and created the United Soviet States of Russia (USSR). After entering into a neutral treaty with Nazi Germany in 1939, the USSR would go on to defeat the Nazi armies once and for all a decade later. Much of what it meant to be on the left in the beginning and middle of the 20th century was your position on the Communist Party of the Soviet Union (CPSU) and the USSR.

France however was occupied by Nazi forces in the 1940s. One of the strongest formations resisting the occupation was the French Communist Party (PCF), which, unlike its Italian counterpart, aligned strongly with the CPSU. As Germany lost ground in the Second World War, the PCF grew more popular and became a significant presence in the French political mainstream, standing in solidarity with the CPSU as it turned on the Nazis and provided a real political alternative to fascism in France. Yet leaked transcripts of speeches made by CPSU officials at a national party congress in 1956 would reveal devastating realities for Russians and citizens throughout the Soviet Union under Joseph Stalin's leadership, who had deployed widespread and deep repression (and an unpopular invasion of Hungary). After a period of gains made by workers throughout Europe and the New World, communists were shaken and asked themselves difficult questions about the revolution that had been so promising in the east. Activists, organizers, and theorists contended with questions about their political strategies, and even more disturbing, their political ideas. What would it mean to be a communist after 1956? To be against capitalism? Over the next fifteen years, the left would lose much of the ground it gained. There began a counter-revolution against gains made by working class peoples throughout the world, both in imperial centers and postcolonial peripheries, each giving birth to new ideas and tactics in struggles against capitalism, white supremacy, colonialism, sexism, and nationalism.

Enter Louis Althusser, a professor of philosophy living in Paris. An ardent PCF member, Althusser did not leave the party after 1956—but he was shaken. So much so that he devoted his career to articulating what it means to be a communist after 1956, when the USSR could not be fully trusted, when the CPSU party line—the ideas of its ideology—warranted skepticism. Examining the most obscure and abstract tenets of communist thinking, he tried to reconcile his commitment to making communism with his disgust at the way communism had been made. He wouldn't leave the party, even after his students and many others did. He didn't leave the party when, during a rare and powerful student uprising and mass strike in 1968, his students took the streets and created a new left that broke with the old. "What use is Althusser?" was spray painted on the walls of a building during these actions. Althusser still stayed with the party when they critiqued the students and workers. He even stayed with the party when its officials pressured his partner Hélène Rytman; he defended her, but kept his membership.

The philosophy Althusser produced between 1960 and 1980 was a definitive rejection of CPSU and PCF official theory. Drawing from a range of influences including the metaphysics of 17th century Jewish Portuguese philosopher Baruch de Spinoza, Italian political philosopher Niccolo Machiavelli, French psychoanalyst Jacques Lacan, Russian revolutionary and theorist V. I. Lenin, Chinese revolutionary activist and philosopher Mao Tse-Tung, French philosopher of science George Canguelheim, and others, Althusser articulated what one of his interpreters would call the most significant intervention in Marxist thinking after 1956. The theory is a thorough rejection of the ideas justifying authoritarian communism, while still maintaining the heart of what it means to be socialist or communist in the Marxist tradition. This philosophy inspired the highest praise and basest ire from intellectuals the world over, especially Western Marxists. It made an impact, shifted the balance of theoretical forces. Just as leftists were confronted with the question of what to think about the CPSU after 1956, for those thinking through the foundations of creating communism and socialism, the question—for a decade or more—was what to think about Althusser.

Alongside the critical theory of the Frankfurt School and postmodernism, Althusserianism (as it was known) became a distinct strand of Marxist thinking that inspired many philosophers and theorists across disciplines in the second half of the 20th century. Just a short list of European and American thinkers Althusser influenced would include Étienne Balibar, Pierre Macherey, Judith Butler, Michel Foucault, Ernesto Laclau, Chantal Mouffe, Stuart Hall, Slavoj Žižek, Anthony Giddens, Jacques Derrida, G. A. Cohen, Jean-Jacques Lecercle, Nicos Poulantzas, Michel Pêcheux, Richard D. Wolff, Stephen Resnick, Jennifer K. Gibson-Graham, and Roy Bhaskar.

Althusser's Life

Althusser's own life is a story of isolation, fame, and deadly scandal. His mother Lucienne Berger fell in love with a man named Louis Althusser, who went to fight with his brother Charles in World War One. The first Louis was a pilot, and was killed in a firefight. Charles, his brother, came back alive and proposed to Lucienne. She accepted and they named their son after her lost love and his lost brother. Charles got a job with the French colonial government service in Algeria, outside of Algiers, where the second Louis was born. A quiet child with a severe father and strong but neurotic mother, Louis excelled in school and passed the French *agrégation*, the most difficult test a teenager can take, granting him admission to the elite *École normale supérieure* in Paris. The year he was supposed to start university World War Two broke out. He enlisted in the army and was quickly taken prisoner when Germany invaded France. Althusser spent four difficult years in a prison camp. As soon as the Nazis were defeated and life returned to relative normalcy, he went back to the *École* and asked if he could start as a first year. The university said yes, and he studied philosophy, beginning a career at that school which would last for thirty years. After he graduated, they hired him as a tutor and lecturer, giving him an apartment at the university in Paris until 1980, when he left in scandal.

Althusser suffered from intense depression. During his time as a student and teacher he was in and out of hospitals, receiving electroshock and psychoanalytic therapy. He would have months-long periods of debilitating mental illness, then periods of manic productivity. In between were volatile symptoms of sadness and active sleepwalking, which sometimes had Althusser walking around his house unconsciously. Nonetheless, he is said to have been an inspiring and generous teacher. During his productive spells, he was extremely prolific and provocative.

Althusser met Hélène Rytman through friends, and though they did not marry for many years, they had a romantic, intellectual, and political connection for decades. Hélène was a communist and intellectual too. An activist with the communist resistance during the Nazi occupation, she saw many of her closest comrades and friends murdered firsthand. She struggled with mental health issues as well. Althusser's relationship with Rytman was fraught, painful for both them, but still somehow nourishing, at least until November 1980. Althusser had been in the hospital and things were at a breaking point between the couple. As Althusser tells it in his memoirs, he woke up giving Hélène a massage one morning in November, as he had done many times before, but rather than the back of her neck he was massaging the front—and she was unconscious. Althusser realized he had killed her, strangled her to death, and ran out of his apartment screaming that he had done it. He was brought to the hospital again, and after an investigation French authorities deemed him unfit to stand trial due to his deteriorated mental health. He was put under house arrest and lived another ten years, writing and being written about.

As the Cold War raged on, Althusser's name fell from grace. As the Berlin Wall fell, so did he. He died in 1990.

His students continued to work through his ideas, however. As is so often the case in philosophy, the theory leads a much different life than its author. This particular theory's impact took a different shape than the man who made it. To these ideas we will soon turn.

Author's Context

Though to some degree the "we" in that sentence means me, David I. Backer, the writer of this text. Mentioning something about my own problematic—my ideological-historical moment, how I have been and am being interpellated, the balance of forces in which I am a subject—is appropriate here.

I was born in Danbury, Connecticut, in the southernmost region of New England, United States of America, in 1984. Ronald Reagan was president. I am white, cishet, middle class, Jewish. My father is a real estate and environmental lawyer specializing in water law, my mother a technical writer for the marketing department of a relocation company. We come from Eastern European immigrants who moved to the United States during the second wave of the 1890s; peasants who made for Brooklyn from Hungary and Prussia.

I didn't have much of a political consciousness until I was a senior in high school on September 11th, 2001. Some of my friends' parents worked in the World Trade Center in New York City, lending a vividness to the attacks. I didn't become critical however until I moved to Quito, Ecuador in 2008, as the financial crisis hit in the North and the Pink Tide flowed in the South. I read Karl Marx seriously for the first time in Quito, watching David Harvey's YouTube lectures on *Capital, Volume One* as I read. I completed a doctorate in philosophy and education in New York City between 2010–2014, where I joined the Occupy Wall Street movement and was active with the Empowerment and Education Working Group. A few years later, I joined the Democratic Socialists of America in May 2016 when Bernie Sanders's presidential candidacy became more than just a dream. I'm now a professor of educational theory living in Philadelphia.

Note on Passages

A note on one of this book's features. I have placed passages—taken from a selection of Althusser's translated writings—throughout the pages. Each passage is in a relevant section of the text, but on its own (and sometimes coupled with related passages). These long quotations are meant to give readers a clearer sense of Althusser's voice and style. Many of these passages come from the early essay collection *For Marx*, *Reading Capital* (the complete edition, published in 2016), and the full book *On the Reproduction of Capitalism*, from which the essay "Ideology and Ideological State Apparatuses: Notes Towards an Investigation", also known as the ISAs essay, was excerpted in 1969. The first chapter on interpellation takes exclusively from *On the Reproduction*, specifically the chapter on ideology. While the ISAs essay has been a popular piece of Althusser's for decades, I recommend that those new to Althusser start with "Is It Simple to Be a Marxist in Philosophy?" This latter essay is a thorough summary of Althusser's philosophy as a whole, which he wrote for a more general audience. A good number of the passages in the book are therefore taken from that essay.

CHAPTER 1

A Beginner's Guide to Interpellation

> We shall go on to suggest that ideology 'acts' or 'functions' in such a way as to 'recruit' subjects among individuals (it recruits them all) or 'transforms' individuals into subjects (it transforms them all) through the very precise operation that we call *interpellation* or *hailing*. It can be imagined along the lines of the most commonplace, everyday hailing...Hailing as an everyday practice governed by a precise ritual takes spectacular form in the police practice of hailing: 'Hey, you there!' (It functions in very similar forms in interpellating or summoning at school.)
> LOUIS ALTHUSSER, *On the Reproduction of Capitalism*, 2014, p. 191

∴

> There are individuals walking along. Somewhere (usually behind them) the hail rings out, 'Hey, you there!' An individual (nine times out of ten, it is the one who is meant) turns around, believing-suspecting-knowing that he's the one—recognizing, in other words, that he 'really is the person' the interpellation is aimed at. In reality, however, things happen *without succession. The existence of ideology and the hailing or interpellation of individuals as subjects are one and the same thing.*
> LOUIS ALTHUSSER, *On the Reproduction of Capitalism*, 2014, p. 191

∴

Getting in Trouble[1]

Everyone gets in trouble. Especially children. My first memory of getting in trouble was at a shopping mall. I was with my father. I think I was four years old. We were getting pizza for lunch after shopping at a children's clothing store called Kids 'R' Us. At the store I saw a keychain I liked. It had a little plastic Batman attached to a short chain. While my father paid for whatever other products we were purchasing, I took the keychain and pocketed it, not knowing—I think—that this was wrong. We went to get pizza.

I had to go to the bathroom, or my father had to go to the bathroom, and we went together. As he was washing his hands at the sink I wanted to show him the keychain. I decided to bring the feet of the plastic figure out of my pocket, showing just the blue boots on gray legs. I said, "Daddy, look, Batman's feet!"

What happened next is blurry. I remember my father seeing the stolen keychain, his eyes widening. He took me back to the toy store, back to the register where I'd taken it, and had me apologize. I remember going home with him in the car, his anger. What I remember most clearly is a feeling. A hot, anxious, nervous feeling—even now I have it when I recall the memory. The sensation is like my stomach and intestines are in boiling water, or the feeling of being outside too long on a hot day. Gut-wrenching.

This feeling was the feeling of being seen by my father, and being the object of his anger. More specifically though, the feeling came from a change: everything went from normal and fine to not normal and not fine, with the added sense that I was the reason for the change. That it was me, in fact, who had done something wrong. My soul turned: I was the one responsible for the change in the situation. I realized that it was me that my father was angry at, for something that I had done with the keychain.

That was when I learned that stealing—not paying for a product at a store with money—is wrong. In our economy, our government, and our culture we pay for things we want with money. We can't just have them or take them if we want them. Even now, when I think about stealing, I have that hot fear, the gut-wrenching feeling from when my father was angry and turned my soul.

I was interpellated. Getting in trouble is a good example of being interpellated. People get into much more serious trouble than what I've just described, and it's just a small example. I was interpellated when I got in trouble, and I got with the program of not stealing. Interpellations like this happen all the time all over the place: family, school, media, sports, shops, government offices. Interpellations get us with the program of daily life in society. They are the concrete moments when we learn to live in our society. Teachable moments.

At School

The first memory I have of getting in trouble at school, though I'm sure there were many, was in first grade. I was seven years old. Mrs. Saunders was our teacher. The room was bright. The sun was shining. I sat in the second or third row at a little pupil desk. Just like all the other students, I looked forward and paid attention to the lesson, whatever it was. Then I picked my nose and ate the mucus.

Mrs. Saunders saw me. She had been on her way to the blackboard, or maybe to her desk at the front of the room. In any case she stopped what she was doing when she saw me. In front of everyone, she faced me. She stopped and turned her shoulders, standing over us at the front of the classroom, and addressed me, just me. The full force of her whole body was oriented right at me. Unlike the moment with my father, I remember exactly what she said:

"David, that is disgusting!"

I even remember the way she said it. She drew out the "dee" sound of the word "disgusting" in a crescendo, which ended with a guttural emphasis on the "guh" sound in the middle of the word. It sounded to me like "deees-GUH-sting!"

I got that feeling again, that transition from okay-to-not okay feeling where I was, in fact, the one who was responsible. My soul turned. This time I had a big audience: my classmates all looked at me. I don't remember their reactions so much as the feeling as being singled out, that it was me, in fact, that Mrs. Saunders was talking about; me, in fact, who was doing something disgusting.

I maybe had been aware that picking my nose and eating it was illicit, unclean, or unhygienic. But I didn't really know it. I learned at that moment, I was interpellated, that we don't to pick our noses and eat it in this society.

Get with the Program

Both the Batman's feet and nose-picking anecdotes show something else. In that soul-turning moment when my gut wrenched because I'd been seen doing something wrong, there was an individual behavior—something I was doing—that society doesn't permit. Essentially, my father and Mrs. Saunders were saying, "David, we don't do that around here. Get with the program." There's a mixture of the individual and collective at this moment, a dissonance when an individual—me, in fact—did something that society—we, us—have decided to prohibit. There's a collectively agreed upon imagined relation to the world that tells us "don't steal" and "don't pick your nose." And there are concrete moments when we learn these things deeply, so that we don't do them anymore.

Other societies at other times or places may not have the same imagined relations, but ours does. We don't steal. We don't pick our noses. I had to learn that our society has a program, that there's a way we do things around here.

Interpellation is a moment of forced integration into that program: when consent to the program gets configured.

I didn't know, but then I learned: we don't take things without paying, we don't pick our noses. The interpellation is the moment someone confronts me to tell me this and it sinks in so that I get with the program. When I believe-suspect-know that I am the one, in fact, who has not understood.

Interpellation is the completed "teachable moment." It's when I go from being an idiot to a citizen, a face in the crowd to a subject of ideology. The soul turns, the gut wrenches, and I now imagine the same relation that others do when it comes to taking things and picking my nose. After the interpellation, I am with the program: my imagination prohibits and permits the things that others' imaginations prohibit and permit.

Not Anything Impactful

An interpellation isn't just something that made an impact on you, or shaped who you are today; not all impactful experiences are interpellations. But all interpellations are impactful experiences, just ones of a certain kind. Sometimes the impact is like a huge boulder falling. Other times, it's like a slow drip that eventually forms a stalagmite. Interpellations leave an impression that orients you to what others do around you, sometimes called norms, patterns of acceptable behavior. The interpellation makes you the kind of person that does the acceptable behavior. It makes it so that acceptable behavior is now part of who you are. It's second nature. To not do it would betray yourself.

You follow the pattern because it—this image—is part of who you are now.

I Don't Remember What I Learned in School

I don't remember exactly what I learned in my classes at school, and it's common to hear this from students studying education: "What was the point of all that school? I don't remember a single thing!"

Yet these comments typically occur in conversations where all kinds of rules, lessons and patterns are occurring to keep the situation going. If you're saying that you don't remember anything from school, you have made a life for yourself within our society based in some part on what you learned in school. For instance, there are a number of things you learned in school that make it possible for you to say—in that way at that moment, politely—that you don't remember what you learned in school.

Why don't we remember what we learned in school, exactly?

First, there's no need to remember because what we learned in school was to become the kind of person that does this and that, which we are doing all the time. It's not just memory of facts that happens in school learning but rather the incorporation of patterns, codes, and expectations which we act out everyday. If we had to remember these things, then school would be less effective at achieving its goal. The point is that you don't have to remember what you learn.

Second, it makes sense that we wouldn't remember these patterns because through interpellations they have become part of ourselves: we are in fact the people that know that 2+2 = 4 and behave in this and that way, because we learned these things at school. It would be like saying, "what's the point of having lungs, I never remember to breathe!" The things we learn at school are second nature, like breathing.

Third, interpellations compose how we see, not just what we see, and it's hard to remember how we're seeing things while we see. I wear glasses, for instance. I rarely remember that what I'm seeing through my glasses are images focused by my glasses. I just see through the glasses and then assume that the world is the way it looks. I don't remember to think about my glasses all the time, I just don't think about them, because they're part of what makes my world appear the way it does. But I'm always wearing them, and I can take them off whenever I want. Or put different ones on when I want.

So it is with what we learn in school through interpellation: the real lessons are the ones we forget because they've been so deeply woven into the fabric of who we are that to remember them would mean that we didn't learn them correctly. The point is to not remember and continue believing.

Testing

The summer of 1994 was a particularly exciting one: I'd be going to a camp for two weeks for the first time, and then traveling with my parents on vacation. I was ten years old.

Earlier that year I took several state-mandated standardized tests in reading, writing, and mathematics. I was in fourth grade. I remember feeling nervous while taking the tests: everything at school stopped, the normal routines and lessons to which I'd grown accustomed ceased and the test became our focus.

On the day of the test our teacher handed out workbooks with the image of the state of Connecticut on the front. The paper was gray, thin, and smelled like grassy pulp. I don't remember the questions themselves, but I do remember looking around and seeing my classmates taking the test also. I remember the time written in chalk on the chalkboard in front of us, alerting us to when we'd started and when we would have to stop. I remember our teacher waiting for us to finish, watching to make sure we didn't cheat. It was a little unpleasant, but largely unmemorable.

After the school year ended, maybe the week after school was over and summer was about to begin, I remember sitting in my room. My mother knocked on the door and asked me to come outside, where our house had a small deck. I followed her. My father was sitting there in shirtsleeves. The sun was strong and my mother sat next to him. In his lap was an envelope with the image of Connecticut on the front. He reached into the envelope and pulled out a single sheet of paper, which had lines of text printed in block letters. There were numbers and words placed next to one another: my state test scores.

My father asked me to come over and look at the piece of paper. I did, and saw that under one of the categories it said "unsatisfactory." He said that if I didn't score higher on such tests in the future, then I wouldn't be allowed to go to summer camp. I remember feeling nervous and confused. It got under my skin. The feeling was a kind of anxious disturbance, a guilt without understanding. It was the first time a state test had affected my life in some way, and I didn't understand why it might be so important that I get certain scores on them. But I did understand that I had to get better scores on them in the future. The same was true for grades.

The test interpellated me in this case: I learned that I had to behave in a certain way with these tests, that around here we perform well on state tests, or else.

Where Did My Friends Go?

I went to a private elementary school from four years old until I was eleven. The school served the wealthier Jewish community in the part of central-western Connecticut where I lived. After I graduated Maimonides Academy, I went to a public middle school, Rogers Park, serving the entire town. Danbury had roughly 60,000 people at that time. A good number of those residents were immigrants and people of color.

Rogers Park had a tracking system for its students. High-performing students with good grades took "honors" level classes, while students with mid-range grades took "regular" classes. There were special education and remedial programs as well.

The public school system can sometimes have difficulties processing information, and the school administration could not confirm that the content I learned at Maimonides met the criteria for the honors level, except for reading and writing. I was put in regular level classes for science, math, and history, and then an honors level literature course (extra classes such as art, home economics, gym, and shop class were exempted from this stratification).

I made good friends in my science classes. I remember them distinctly. I was close to Enrique and Josè. They had brown skin, and spoke with accents inflected with Latin American Spanish. I saw them in most of my classes, except for literature, where there were other students I met named Jeff, Chris, and Andrew. These students had the pinkish color of skin known as white.

But race is only one social category. A friend of mine in math named James had white skin, but lived in a small house a few miles from me. His father was a truck driver and his mother had an illness and could not work. I remember his Rottweiler dog. I don't remember going to Enrique or José's houses, and have only one memory of José coming to my house. (I don't know if this imbalance in visiting houses was intentional.) Andrew and Jeff, however, lived in bigger houses. Their parents were doctors and businesspeople.

In seventh grade I was moved to honors science classes, as well as honors history. The mistake with my grades from Maimonides had been corrected. I saw my friends Enrique and José less and less, and saw people like Andrew and Jeff more and more. Interestingly, I saw James some more and spent time with another white friend, whose father was a construction worker, Mike.

But by then I'd noticed the change, and wondered, with a light sense of confusion that I never raised with anyone nor did anyone raise it with me, where Enrique and José had gone. They weren't in the honors level classes.

The sense of confusion about their disappearance from my life, through the subtle neglect created when no one asks, settled into a kind of obviousness and normality. Again, there was a change. This transition was not gut-wrenching, but yet my soul turned: I learned that people like Enrique and José, and increasingly people like James, were not, in fact, the kind of students in honors classes. I was the kind of person that was in honors classes, like Andrew and Jeff.

This remained true throughout high school, where I sometimes saw my former friends passing in the hallway. We barely recognized each other. We didn't say hello. When I went off to a private university in Washington, DC, I was not surprised to see that most people there were not like my friends in the sixth grade, when the public school had made a mistake.

To say that I wasn't surprised at university isn't really correct. Being surprised assumes that you're actually thinking about something, expecting it, and then something different happens. I wasn't actually thinking about the kind of person who attended classes with me at college or high school. I wasn't expecting that people with different skin colors and different access to resources than mine would or wouldn't be present. I just didn't think about it.

The tracking system had interpellated me in this case. It had turned my soul so that I didn't think about race and class stratifications, and how schools reproduce them. I learned that it wasn't something to think about.

Falling in Love

Interpellation isn't only a gut-wrenching, difficult, unpleasant moment. It's also deeply personal. The theorist Mladen Dolar says that it's like falling in love.

I fell in love with my partner at a bar. It was our first date. I didn't know I was falling in love but when I think about it now that's when it happened. We'd been dancing bachata, a South American dance. The date had been going well, better than most dates I'd been on at that time. We took a break from the dance floor. I sat on a stool, ordered us two drinks, and she put her arm around my neck and leaned on me. Her hand rested on my collar bone, a friendly gesture. She didn't say anything, just put her arm around me and waited for the beers, listening to the music. It was so intimate. That's when I fell in love with her, if I had to guess. It was a transformational feeling, as though my inner life were a galaxy and there was a shift in the gravitational forces between the parts of myself. This person had arrived. When she put her arm around me I remember thinking to myself "who are you?" Something transformed within me. The physical space was the same. The bar was the bar, the stool was the stool, but I was no longer what I had been. There was something new about me and what was new about me was this person. There was a shift, a movement. I was moved. I became so interested in this person that I shifted my life significantly around her. If someone were to ask me who I am, for example, pretty soon I'd start talking about her.

People sometimes describe the process of establishing this deep connection 'falling in' love. I don't know why we say that. Maybe we fall because there is such a significant change, a reorientation of who we are, that it's outside our control. Like we're falling. But we always fall in love with someone: there's another person there. It's this other person who shifts our inner life so significantly, and the sense of the depth of that connection, is like a gravitational force.

For some psychologists, love names how we become who we are: babies fall in love with their parents and through this process develop personalities that inherit and reject certain of their features. This process of incorporating features and elements from our surroundings doesn't stop either. It keeps going, all the time.

There are things other than love that we can 'fall into.' Falling is a metaphor. We can also fall into ideology—that's an interpellation. While falling in love isn't an interpellation itself, being interpellated is like the experience of falling in love.

> When religious ideology begins to function directly by interpellating the little child Louis as a subject, little Louis is already-subject—not yet religious subject, but familial subject. When legal ideology (later, let us suppose) begins to interpellate little Louis by talking to him about, not Mama and Papa now, or God and the Little Lord Jesus, but Justice, he was already a subject, familial, religious, scholastic, and so on...Finally, when, later, thanks to auto-heterobiographical circumstances of the type Popular Front, Spanish Civil War, Hitler, 1940 Defeat, captivity, encounter with a communist, and so on, political ideology (in its different forms) begins to interpellate the now adult Louis as a subject, he has already long been, always-already been, a familial, moral, religious, scholastic, and legal subject...This political subject begins, once back from captivity, to make the transition from traditional Catholic activism to advanced—semi-heretical—Catholic activism, then begins reading Marx, then joins the Communist Party, and so on. So life goes. (Althusser, *On the Reproduction of Capitalism*, 2014, p. 193)

> ...we shall point out that these practices are regulated by rituals in which they are inscribed, within the material existence of an ideological apparatus, even if it is just a small part of that apparatus: a small mass in a small church, a funeral, a minor match at a sport club, a school day or a day of classes at university, a meeting or rally of a political party...Pascal says, more or less, 'Kneel down, move your lips in prayer, *and you will believe.*' (Althusser, *On the Reproduction of Capitalism*, 2014, p. 186)

Is Interpellation Passive?

Interpellation makes it seem like there's something that is being done to us. It seems like we are passive creatures that receive the social order, which is active. It's tempting to say society interpellates us, and that "I was interpellated by society." But we are actively doing things to be interpellated. We learn. And it isn't clear at all who or what interpellates. Certainly my father, Mrs. Saunders, the Connecticut state test, and the tracking system at Rogers Park interpellated me. But what are they, exactly?

They are the bearers of a structure that they maintain through their actions. In saying and doing what they said and did, they reproduced imagined relations to real conditions. Both in the sense of giving birth and in the sense carrying, they were bearers of a social structure immanent in its effects.

Ideology = Imagined Relations to Real Conditions

Interpellations are all about ideology. Ideology is a representation of imagined relations to real conditions. Real conditions are the complex layers of stuff that make up reality. Having an imagined relationship to the real conditions means imagining that this complex reality is one or way or another, that it's "cut and dry" or "is what it is," and then acting accordingly.

When someone says "well, it is what it is," then you know they're talking about an ideology. The ideology is a kind of guarantee where there really isn't any guarantee.

Reality is always more complicated than how ideology alludes.

Ideology presents a world that people extract from reality for certain reasons. People allude to the way things are in speech and action: this allusion is an ideology. They're not under an illusion, but rather are alluding to a world that is never as complex as reality. They allude to their imagined relation to the real conditions, which is never just "their" individual relation, but rather the social structure's.

Wings

Every time an interpellation happens, an ideology gets it wings.

Race and Gender

Althusser rarely, if ever, wrote about race and gender. It's a serious flaw in his work. But his ideas can be applied to race and gender. Race, for example, is a relation between people imagined with physical or cultural features (skin color, body type, language). The real conditions are that people are different in certain ways, but race imagines these differences immanently through a set of practices, all of which form a sort of caste system. Gender too: people with certain reproductive organs should look and behave in certain ways (be manly, be lady-like), should love certain people, etc.

People get interpellated into their race. They get interpellated into their gender. The interpellations vary, and happen in distinctive ways in different contexts. Race and gender are imagined relations to real conditions (which means they're not necessarily identities).

Reproduction

Interpellations reproduce ideologies. Reproducing means creating anew, maintaining, continuing, perpetuating. It's like biological reproduction: living things create themselves anew when they reproduce. They maintain the existence of their species. They continue the passage of their traits and genes.

Reproduction is making sameness during changing circumstances.

Schools are one of the most important sites of interpellations: they tend to reproduce society as it is, but can also reproduce other kinds of societies too.

Consent

Interpellations configure consent to ideologies. But this consent isn't express consent. No one rationally consents to the social structure through an interpellation. Rather, an interpellation is a process of configuring a kind of unconscious tacit consent, which might develop into express consent (if the ruling classes are lucky).

Individuality

We aren't born knowing we are individuals, we must learn to become individuals by being told that we are individuals. We're interpellated as individuals and we become individuals when those around us and our environment allude to our individuality. Isn't it funny that, because of society, we're all individuals?

> However, while admitting that these ideologies do not correspond to reality and, accordingly, constitute an *illusion*, we also admit that they do make *allusion* to reality and that we need only 'interpret' them to discover the reality of this world beneath the surface of their imaginary representation of it (ideology = illusion/allusion). (Althusser, *On the Reproduction of Capitalism*, 2014, p. 181)

> *THESIS I:* Ideology represents individuals' imaginary relation to their real conditions of existence. (Althusser, *On the Reproduction of Capitalism*, 2014, p. 181)

Images

You can't see your own eyes. While you can see sunsets and movies and taxi cabs with your eyes, your eyes can't see themselves as they are. Even if you took out your own eye and looked at it, that would be one of your eyes looking the other (and it's not clear that the eye you've taken out is still your eye). You can see a reflection of your eye, but this is only a reflection, not the eye itself. This eye-seeing problem is a big problem for humans. Your eye is the thing that sees, but because it's the thing that sees, it will never see itself like it sees other things.

If you think about your eye as if it were a person, personify your eye, they would be a tragic figure: always trying to see but never able to see themselves.

Well, it would only be a tragedy if this person wanted to see everything, including themselves, or took a particular interest in seeing themselves. But as babies, humans are exactly this way: wanting to see and discover. At a certain point, in the first six months of life, a baby wants to see themselves, but they can't. Frustrated, they look around wondering if other things are themselves and find other people and objects and creatures. In this phase, they are constantly asking, without language, "is that me?"

Anything will do to answer this urgent question. Faces, voices, objects, reflections. All of these partially answer the question, but never in full. So it never works, fully. Only partially. Just as the eye can't see itself, the self cannot know itself. I'm not the reflection I see in the mirror. I'm not the people around me. I can't know fully who I am. The baby sees their parents, familiar objects and people, their own reflection in a mirror. They say, "yes, that must be me." That sentence of consolation, it must be me, and turns into a kind of thought, layering into what becomes the ever-expanding thought about the self. The "it" in "it must be me" is a presentation, a painting done by the senses and drives, added to a gallery engaged in a never-ending exhibition called Who I Am. "It," or the thing that I must be, is a portrait of a moment, a memory in color. One way that we incorporate categories like race, gender, and class is through these portraits.

The search continues well into adulthood. People are always sort of asking this question, answering it to themselves by painting a portrait of whatever they find and adding it to the collection. They're images. The images emerge from relations to the real conditions of existence. Images and relations together are ideology itself: imagined relations. Interpellations happen because of this constant searching for an answer to the question. An interpellation adds images to the collection. Interpellations happen because we're always open to them, always asking who we are and never getting the full answer.

Before going to a party, I look in the mirror to see how I look. I'm always frustrated by the fact that my appearance is reversed in the mirror, that people never see me the way I see myself in the mirror and that I can't know how I look to others. I can't see myself in the way that I'll be seen, always having to settle for a reversed reflection. But the problem is too difficult to solve so I just believe the image: yes, that's how I look. Fine.

But it's not. I go the party anyway, consciously satisfied but still unconsciously wondering.

Being Guided

Because the images make up the self, they're related to how the self makes decisions. Certain images become "should" images and others "should not" images. When the self follows the should and should not images it's being guided by those images. Althusser says that we go all by ourselves with ideology, which means that we make free choices, as subjects, with our subjectivities configured to make those free choices. But because we don't know every part of ourselves, specifically how we are subjects in the social structure, we are guided by things we don't know about. Ideology isn't consciousness. It's unconscious.

Interpellation Machine

Imagine a machine. It's about the height of a person. It looks like a coat rack, with a box-like head on top of a spine, and legs holding it steady on the bottom. The machine's "head," or top part, is a set of very thin picture frames connected by rails along their sides. There are thousands of them stacked together very tightly. There's a cage-like structure holding these frames to the spine. It contains the frames and it's spring-loaded such that the frames, when deployed, extend outward sort of like one of those joke boxing gloves at the end of an extending coat rack. When a trigger is pulled, the rail-and-frames spring out.

The machine moves in this way: a frame in the cage shoots out from the others in a certain direction, extending on an arm, so it's still connected to the machine because of the rails. The frame comes out at you from the cage, like a blank painting on a wall that wants you to be in it and starts to chase you. The machine is secured somewhat to a wall, or some structure, but it also has wheels so it can amble around.

The frames aren't empty. They have a translucent, putty-like substance that's pliable and flexible, like a thin clay, that can capture the features of whatever it makes contact with. At first, the substance is wet and shapeable in the cage, like new concrete. But after it makes contact with whatever it aims to capture, the substance hardens, like concrete setting. It's not as hard as concrete, more like the tough rubber on a plunger or a thick rubber band.

So the machine sends out a frame of shapeable rubber in some direction, to capture something, typically a person's face, but it could be a non-human object too. It lets the arm linger on this target for just long enough to take an impression of it. Then the arm retracts back, so the frame, now hardened into a rubber portrait-impression of the target, returns to the cage.

There's a second part of the process.

On the other side of the cage with the empty frames waiting to go outwards, there is another cage. This second cage, attached to the other side of the spine, contains a complex amalgam of hardened rubber impressions, the results of the frame-catch process completed by the other side of the machine.

The rubber impressions are all grafted and layered onto one another. This combination of rubber impressions looks like a twisted ball-square, a polygon made of faces, words, places, objects…all smashed into one another so that the objects themselves maintain much of their original features, but also get stretched or compacted, distorted, as they become part of the mass. This second cage is slightly heated to keep the rubber pliable. The resulting bolus is like a terribly-made spherical cake, having no distinct form except the ever-changing and idiosyncratic mass emerging when piling rubber impressions one on top of the other and heating them.

The entire process of the interpellation machine: A frame goes out and takes the impression of its target, the machine retraces the frame back to the first cage, but then a series of little mechanical arms grab the rubber impression, now hardened, and pass it back to the second cage, where another set of arms add the new impression to the bolus. That's an interpellation. The whole thing buzzes. Imagine billions of these machines reaching out and framing and incorporating stuff around them into themselves, both other machines and stuff from their surroundings, each machine with idiosyncratic boluses resulting from the stuff they happen to frame and incorporate. That's ideology, reproducing.

Intersectionality

People end up having races, genders, species, classes, abilities, religions, and nationalities. Any given interpellation has these categories riding it. Multiple categories. The categories will be ordered in a certain way, with primary and secondary and tertiary salience, and the categories will mix with one another like chemicals or ingredients such that the interpellation will be idiosyncratic for each individual to become subject to the ideology. Intersectionality names the myriad ways one social structure can conjure its single relation of production among such difference.

Counter-Interpellation

Not all interpellations are successful. For an interpellation to succeed, there has to be an imagined relation to real conditions. There also has to be someone who hasn't gotten with the program. In a concrete moment, the person has to believe-suspect-know that they're the ones who aren't with the program. Then they get with the program. But a lot has to happen for this to be successful. It doesn't always work. A lot of times, people just don't get it (this has been called misinterpellation by the theorist James Martel). Other times, people are in between interpellations and are neither interpellated nor not interpellated (philosopher of education Tyson E. Lewis calls this disinterpellation). And sometimes, people consciously or unconsciously change the program.

When someone takes up and takes on an ideology in a concrete moment to shift the balance of forces in its social formation, that's what the French philosopher of language Jean-Jacques Lecercle calls a counter-interpellation. Think of the phrase "against the grain." This saying refers to the grain of wood, or the direction of the fibers in the wood. These fibers go a certain way such that it's easier to cut the wood when you cut in that direction. Cutting against this direction increases resistance and friction. At first it might seem like a counter-interpellation is just something that goes against the grain of society. But taking up and taking on an ideology to shift the balance of forces in a social formation has to have the potential to change that balance of forces. The counter-interpellation has to be able to change the very grain of the wood, not just go against that grain. Resisting is going against the grain. Counter-interpellating is changing the grain.

A Grain of Sand

You can also use the word grain to refer to individual pieces of matter, like a grain of sand. A completed interpellation is like dropping a grain of sand on a beach. The grain comes to rest in either a big, well-developed pile or becomes part of a small heap. After millions of interpellations over time a topography develops with contours and high mounds and ditches. If enough counter-interpellations happen against the predominant balance of forces in a pile, the topography can change.

Society is like a beach in this metaphor, or layers of rock. It has a complex structure that shifts all the time, grains moving this way and that, each having tiny effects which accumulate into other bigger effects that then turn into volcanic eruptions, tectonic shifts, and the creation of continents. There are higher and lower positions; variations of grains that predominate over others; shifts and stabilizations that are more or less likely in that particular balance of forces. Society has a structure like this.

There are different forces in the structure that we can point to. One force keeps the existing structure the way it is (a "top-down," repressive, superstructure force). Another force roots the structure (a "bottom-up" base force), arranging the grains and levels and regions in a certain way. Each of these forces continue forward in time, reproducing themselves until something changes. Personify the grains so that each grain imagines how it relates to other grains around it and the entire formation—that imagined relation is ideology.

> ...every social formation 'functions on ideology,' in the sense in which one says that a gasoline engine 'runs on gasoline.' (Althusser, *On the Reproduction of Capitalism*, 2014, p. 200)

> We can now say the following. It is characteristic of the Ideological State Apparatuses that they form part of the superstructure and, as such, ensure the reproduction of the relations of production behind the protective shield of the Repressive State Apparatus...However, since they ensure the reproduction of the relations of production in the 'consciousness' of subjects who are agents of production, agents of exploitation, and so on, we have to add that this reproduction of the relations of production by the Ideological State Apparatuses and their ideological effects on subjects...is ensured *in* the functioning of the relations of production themselves. (Althusser, *On the Reproduction of Capitalism*, 2014, p. 201)

> The base is dominated by the relations of production. The relations of production function (on the basis, of course, of material labour processes that produce objects of social utility as commodities) simultaneously as...relations of exploitation. (Althusser, *On the Reproduction of Capitalism*, 2014, p. 202)

Hut

Societies aren't like beaches or layers of earth exactly though, since they're made and maintained for certain purposes according to certain interests. The English philosopher G. A. Cohen says that another metaphor for a society could be a hut.

The repressive force is like a roof, holding things in place from the top down. This roof represents government, police, military, law, and court systems. This force is how society makes sure its structure doesn't fall down, and keeps the rain and sun out.

The base or bottom-up force that arranges that layout of the hut is like the floor and basement. This floor represents the economy, or modes of production. It's the way the society is rooted to the earth, connecting/using/tackling/working with ecological forces without which the society couldn't function.

The middle of the hut, or the posts and walls, are where we live: it's where family, school, culture, sports, media, religion all happen. It's covered by the government overhead and supported by the economy below. The middle region is also the thing that people experience directly, and helps to maintain consent to living in a hut with a certain kind of roof and foundation.

Ideologies are the imagined relations to the hut's design and daily routines: how it should be designed, maintained, and fashioned. Ideologies are how people go all by themselves as they live within the walls of the society. Interpellations are those teachable moments when we learn to live in the hut and keep it going: when we get with the hut's program.

A Play

The best metaphor for society would be a combination of the beach and the hut. A play does this. In a play, there is no single author, yet there is a clear series of roles that combine to form the action. There is also a house-like structure, the theater. Society, Althusser says, is like an authorless theater.

Our Society: Capitalism and Democracy

Our society in the United States, very generally speaking at least, has a capitalist economy for its base and a representative democratic government for its roof. Our culture is a complex mess of religions, nationalities, musics, foods, and routines.

United States capitalism is an economic arrangement where a relatively few people own most resources privately, and these few pay everyone else to work for them. Capitalists and workers, whether they can feel it or not, are always fighting with each other to get more for themselves. Stuff in this social formation, like nature and human labor, are worth some amount of money and are exchanged in markets. In capitalism, to make a living, you have to work for money. This a noble scam: the amount of value you generate by working is always more than you get paid to do it. The situation couldn't be otherwise if someone else pays you work. You then have to buy things you need with money. This is all very competitive. The few who own most resources compete with each other to make the most money, while most people compete for opportunities to make enough money to live. It's up to individuals, who are "free" to compete in this setting, to make their lives together. It's possible in principle for anyone to be very rich in this arrangement, but unlikely that anyone in particular will be rich or even well taken care of. There's great wealth and poverty, with most people in the second category but always hoping to be in the first, while some have benefited from compromises made with the wealthy. Debt is everywhere. Sometimes the people who work for the people that own everything get together and demand better pay and working conditions. These are unions. Sometimes they strike to make sure the capitalists know they mean business. Only 11% of workers are unionized in the US, and this number is shrinking.

The government tries to provide some measure of help to workers. Since there are local, state, and federal governments the United States, the country has multiple repressive state apparatuses. Each of these have executive, legislative, and judicial branches by which decisions are made and implemented. We elect officials to each level of government, who then appoint officials to other posts that make our government run. We have a partially social-democratic arrangement where government provides services to citizens using tax dollars. These services include schools, infrastructure, libraries, transportation, housing, a version of healthcare, social security. Recently, these programs have been weakened. We also have the largest most powerful military in the world, on which we spend a good amount of our public money, as well as a police force that uses military tactics and resources.

The culture emerging from, reproducing, and resisting our government and economy is complex. There's urban/suburban/rural geography; Christian/non-Christian/secular religious belief; multiple heritages in slavery, colonialism, imperialism; male/female/intersex hierarchies; levels of education; access and usage of technology. Interpellations configure consent to the imagined relations to real conditions that keep this theater running. But the elements and variations and their forces in this social formation are always shifting: it could always be otherwise.

> When nothing is happening, the Ideological State Apparatuses have worked to perfection. When they no longer manage to function, to reproduce the relations of production in the 'consciousness' of all subjects, 'events' happen, as the phrase goes, more or less serious events…With, at the end, some day or the other, after a long march, the revolution. (Althusser, *On the Reproduction of Capitalism*, 2014, p. 206)

Note

1 This chapter was written as a pamphlet for student teachers and activists studying interpellation (and sometimes philosophy) for the first time.

CHAPTER 2

The Law of Dislocation

> What interested me above all else in Marx's text was his radical double opposition to empiricism and to Hegel. In opposition to empiricism, Marx argued that knowledge does not proceed from the concrete to the abstract but from the abstract to the concrete...I quote *'in thought,'* while the real object, which gives rise to this whole process, exists outside thought. In opposition to Hegel, Marx argued that this movement from the abstract to the concrete was not a manner of producing reality but of coming to know it. And what fascinated me in all this argument was that *one had to begin with the abstract.*
>
> LOUIS ALTHUSSER, *Philosophy and the Spontaneous Philosophy of the Scientists and Other Essays, Is it Simple to be a Marxist in Philosophy?*, 1990a, p. 226

∴

> Thus I arrived at my thesis: if the process of knowledge does not transform the real object, but only transforms its perception into concepts and then into a thought-concrete, and if all this process takes place, as Marx repeatedly points out, *'in thought,' and not in the real object*, this means that, with regard to the real object, in order to know it, 'thought' operates on the transitional forms which designate the real object in the process of transformation in order finally to produce a concept of it, the thought-concrete.
>
> LOUIS ALTHUSSER, *Philosophy and the Spontaneous Philosophy of the Scientists and Other Essays, Is it Simple to be a Marxist in Philosophy?*, 1990a, p. 228

∴

Concrete-Real vs. Concrete-in-Thought

Sunset. The word makes so much sense it seems strange to analyze it. What's a sunset? To us, the sun falls below the horizon. But the sun does no such thing. While we keep the concept of sunset, we also know that our planet revolves around the sun so that it illuminates different sides of the earth while others experience night. According to this revolution theory, there's no such thing as a sunrise or sunset. The planet revolves and its position with respect to the sun changes. To beings on earth, however, the sun looks like it's setting and rising. We're beings on earth and name it thus. The English language retains the concept of sunrise, and we use it again and again so it retains its meaning. English speakers learn the word sunset and use the word sunset while also learning that, in reality, there's no such thing.

There's a thing in the head, which is in reality, and a thing in reality (that isn't in the head). The thing in the head is about the thing in reality, but the thing in reality isn't identical to the thing in the head. They're separate. In the case of the sunset, we make a mistake: we assume that the concept we have of what's happening with the sun is in reality what's happening with the sun. We call it a sunset, but the sun doesn't set. There are real conditions of the sun's movement. We imagine a relation to those conditions and then make a swap of one for the other. A mental sleight of hand.

The lesson here isn't a gotcha moment. It seems like the lesson should be: the sun may look like it sets, but—gotcha—it doesn't really set. Rather (continues the gotcha moment), the earth really revolves around the sun, which makes the sun look like it's setting, and so the word sunset doesn't refer to anything. But this isn't the lesson of the sunset. The lesson isn't that one theory of sunsets is the real theory which explains what's happening once and for all, making it cut and dry. The lesson is that there are two separate items that a mental sleight of hand hides: on the one hand, there's a complex reality when it comes to the sun and the earth and time and planetary movement and humans' position viz. all this, and on the other hand there's the theory of that complex reality. The sleight of hand will make it look like the thing in the head—Keplerian or not—is really the thing in the world; that the movement of planets is really a revolving movement. Even in the case of the second theory, the Keplerian version of things, it's possible to make the same sleight of hand: that the earth rotates around the sun. The theory of revolution is about the complex system of planetary movement, yes, but it's another thing to further think that the theory of rotation is what's really happening. Again, you might say that the earth really does rotate around the sun and that's why it looks like a sunset, and this sunset is really an earthturn, but the earthturn—like sunset—is another word that's part of a theory imagining a relation to the complex system of planetary movement.

The word to think about most carefully in this statement is the word really. What is real? The real conditions are complex and lend themselves to multiple imagined relations, ones that serve different purposes. Humans disagree and struggle over answers to these questions and, for political reasons, some imagined relations win out over others. It took hundreds of years for the Catholic Church to pardon Galileo for claiming the earth revolved around the sun. He died under house arrest in 1642. The church admitted he was right in 1992.

In the United States, climate change is another example: whether humans are causing the climate to warm is very much a political question. There are people who benefit a great deal from an imagined relation to real conditions that doesn't blame human activity for climate change. The real conditions of climate change are indeed complex, and they are always dislocated from the images humans have about it. We know because the climate change deniers have power, and the term has been banned in certain states. The facts get established by struggle in addition to observation. The people with the things in their heads fight it out, the real conditions being what they are, and someone wins.

There are at least two real things involved when talking about theories of sunsets, or theories about anything. The first thing is what Althusser called the concrete-real, or what the 17th century Portuguese philosopher Baruch de Spinoza called the world of things. The concrete-real is the system of planetary movement: stuff, reality. But there is a certain kind of concrete-real that's in the head: a concrete-in-thought. The concrete-in-thought is a thing in reality, but one of its distinctive qualities is that it's about other concrete-reals. A concrete-in-thought is a thing in the world too, but it's a thing in the head about other concrete-real stuff in the world.

Just the term concrete-real already points to a decision about reality: the concrete-real is real, it's in the world of things. There's an object that's part of the world of things (complex system of planetary movement) and an object that's also part of the world of things about the world of things (rotation theory, the words sunset and earthturn). According to the law of dislocation, the two are always in separate tracks, separate rooms, separate lines. The concrete-in-thought is dislocated from the concrete-real, but they're both things in the world. The dislocation is twofold: when it comes to what we know, the concrete-in-thought is dislocated from the concrete-real; when it comes to what there is, the concrete-real is dislocated from the concrete-in-thought. The concrete-in-thought is never located in the concrete-real. Thoughts and things are both real but they're not the same.

In other words, the concrete-in-thought is about the concrete-real, but it isn't out and about.

The mental sleight of hand mentioned before skips the law of dislocation, obscuring the difference between the world of ideas and the world things. The sleight of hand is a thing in the head that poses or hides as a thing in the world, a hubristic and trickster concrete-in-thought claiming that it's a concrete-real. This mental sleight of hand locates the concrete-in-thought in the concrete-real and tries to tell you that the sun is really setting, or the earth is really turning.

> The theoretical problematic underlying this text allows us to distinguish Marxist philosophy from every speculative or empiricist philosophy. The decisive point of Marx's thesis concerns the principle distinguishing between the *real* and *thought*. The real is one thing, along with its different aspects: the real-concrete, the process of the real, the real totality, etc. *Thought* about the real is another, along with its different aspects: the thought process, thought-totality, the thought-concrete, etc. (Althusser, Balibar, Establet, Macherey, & Rancière, *Reading Capital: The Complete Edition*, 2016, p. 232)

Snakes, Ropes, and Concepts

Ancient Hindu texts mention a man who walked into a dark room containing a coil of rope and a candle. He thought the rope was a snake and stepped on it. He was incorrect. There was a concrete-real, the rope, and a concrete-in-thought, the snake. The concrete-in-thought is inadequate to the real conditions. But even if the man knew it was a rope, even it was adequate, his concept would still be a concrete-in-thought about a concrete-real. Just because the concept is adequate for the real conditions doesn't mean that the concept is out there in the real conditions. Concepts are things about other things. Things in the world and things in the head are like parallel lines that never converge but follow similar vectors: one is never in the other's place, but they are related in important ways.

Althusser's understanding of concepts isn't like others.' Concepts are concretes-in-thought. Concepts are things, which means that they undergo processes of transformation: they're the product of work. Concepts come from somewhere. They're made through labor processes which occur under certain circumstances. Althusser distinguished between three kinds of concepts, or generalities. Generality I is an existing concept, like a received idea or common sense. Generality II is a concept, like a method, that does some kind of work on concepts. Generality III is a Generality I that has undergone some process of transformation. Someone worked on a Generality I using a Generality II and made a Generality III. Any concrete-in-thought was at one point part of common sense. Then someone used some method of thinking and made that common sense into another concept, which maybe at some point could become common sense again until others use a method of thinking to transform it, etc. Althusser called this process of transforming concepts theoretical practice.

At first glance it might seem like the law of dislocation—the concrete-in-thought is about the concrete-real, but it isn't out and about—is what philosophers of science call anti-realism, which says more or less that scientific knowledge is never fully objectively right or wrong about the world. Realists will say, in response, that if we predict events accurately, create technologies that function, and prove the same results over and over again, that the concepts and the reality match up and we know the truth. Anti-realists say no, not really, our ideas are just adequate to reality, but we never know the truth about reality in the way the realists claim. The law of dislocation sounds like a rejection of realism, but it's actually a kind of realism since it still claims there's a reality that we can know about (the concrete-real). More importantly though, Althusser's understanding of concepts as material things in the head that have undergone and do undergo processes of transformation sets the law of dislocation apart. The man who thought the rope was a snake had something in his head that came from somewhere: perhaps he lives in a region where snakes are feared and prevalent; maybe he had a traumatic experience with a snake as boy and is on the lookout for snakes; perhaps he was raised in a household that worshipped snakes, was interpellated to that culture, and he renounced that religion. Whatever the case, his concrete-in-thought configured his relation to the real conditions of that room so that he saw a snake. And even if he knew it was a rope, the concept of rope also would have come from somewhere, started out as a common sense and been produced through a method. Just as his concept of snake wasn't located in that room next to the candle, neither would his concept of rope, had he thought it. The concept rope is never coiled. This is why Althusser cites Spinoza's aphorism that the concept dog doesn't bark. The concrete-real is parallel with the concrete-in-thought, which encounters other concretes-in-thought as part of the world of things—though the two never meet.

> The fact that [atoms] are *parallel*, that here everything is an effect of parallelism, recalls Epicurus' rain. The attributes fall in the empty space of their determination like raindrops that can undergo encounters only in this exceptional parallelism *without encounter or union* (of body and soul...) known as man, in this assignable but minute parallelism of thought and the body, which is still only parallelism, since, here as in all

> things, 'the order and connection of ideas is the same as the order and connection of things.' In sum, a *parallelism without encounter*, yet a parallelism that is already, in itself, *encounter* thanks to the very structure of the relationship between the different elements of each attribute... Thought is simply the succession of the modes of attribute 'thought,' and refers us, not to a Subject, but, as good parallelism requires, to the succession of the modes of the attribute 'extension.' (Althusser, *Philosophy of the Encounter: Later Writings, 1978–1987*, 2006, p. 178)

The Gold and the Dross

For Spinoza, thought and extension are different attributes of the one infinite substance. They're part of the same universe but always distinct attributes. Likewise, concepts and reality are always parallel in the two ways mentioned before. They're parallel when it comes to what we know and they're parallel when it comes to what there is. The law of dislocation claims both. Saying the concrete-in-thought is never located in the concrete-real, or that the concepts are not located in reality (that they're about reality but never out and about) means that there's a difference between what Althusser called the real object and the object of knowledge. RO ≠ OK. This formula is the full law of dislocation.

The real object is a concrete-real: stuff and things. The object of knowledge is a concrete-in-thought: a concept. Though both are objects, and one is about the other, they are never the same, and one is never located in the other. They are dislocated.

Althusser uses an an analogy for dislocation, gold and dross. Gold is a substance found in layers of sediment, or dross. Before you pan for gold, or mine it, the gold is part of the dross, woven into the rock. It can be removed, extracted from the dross, which most people really want to do because gold is valuable. Dross is the rest, a byproduct that just happened to contain the gold. Dross is a mess. It's structured, but complex. It's made of a variety of elements which pressure one another uniquely, layered with staggering and zigzagging edges, where certain forces work in particular ways on particular elements and variations of elements. Gold however is one element among many. Humans value it and look for it so they can enrich themselves. We isolate and extract and trade it, measure it. We take gold from the dross. The dross, most times, is just a means towards the gold.

To Althusser, the relationship between the real object (concrete-real) and object of knowledge (concrete-in-thought) is like the relationship between gold and dross. The real object, reality, is complexly layered and structured. It's a mess, but not entirely beyond comprehension. People take knowledge out of reality and use it. The knowledge is sort of there in the reality, but only if you're looking for it, and that knowledge is only one facet of the structured sedimentary whole of reality. Only certain humans with certain interests extract gold from dross. Apply the analogy to knowledge and reality and you get the law of dislocation.

But the above, the law of dislocation, is just one way to think about gold and dross. Some people focus on the gold, which means they only think about the dross to get the gold. Once they get the gold they forget about the dross. Some people even think that gold is the truth of dross since it's the most valuable to human economies. To people that think this way, the gold is the highest form of the dross: gold is the essence of dross because it's so prized. The dross in this case is just a changing set of complications that we must sort through to get the gold.

Others think: gold is there in the dross and we know it's there because we observe it, period. Certainly the gold is there whether we look for it or not— we can observe it. Through perception we have a direct relationship with the nature of the dross so that we can see the gold is there, obviously. This is unproblematic (says this second group), and if you take issue with saying that gold is naturally present in the dross then you're unscientific. Naturally, the gold is there. Anything that can't be observed shouldn't be considered scientifically relevant.

Each of these ways of thinking about gold and dross represent a theory, each of them the result of a theoretical practice and each having a theoretical practice unique to them. Althusser calls them Marxist, Hegelian (or expressive or speculative), and empiricist theories respectively. The first theory follows the law of dislocation while the second two don't, but in different ways.

> The whole empiricist process of knowledge lies in fact in an operation of the subject called *abstraction*. To know is to abstract from the real object its essence, the possession of which by the subject is then called knowledge. Whatever particular variants this concept of abstraction may adopt, it defines an invariant structure which constitutes the specific index of empiricism. Empiricist abstraction, which abstracts from the given *real* object its essence, is a *real abstraction*, leaving the subject in possession of the *real* essence. We shall see that this repetition at every moment of the process of the category *real* is characteristic of the empiricist conception. What does a *real* abstraction actually mean? It accounts for what is declared to be a real fact: the essence is abstracted from real objects

> in the sense of an *extraction*, as one might say the gold is *extracted* (or abstracted, i.e., separated) from the dross of earth and sand in which it is held and contained. Just as gold, before its abstraction, exists as gold unseparated from its dross in the dross itself, so the essence of the real exists as a real essence *in* the real which contains it.
>
> *The real*: it is structured as a dross of earth containing inside it a grain of pure gold, i.e., it is made of two real essences, the pure essence and the impure essence, the gold and the dross, or, if you like (Hegelian terms), the essential and inessential. (Althusser, Balibar, Establet, Macherey, & Rancière, *Reading Capital: The Complete Edition*, 2016, pp. 35–36)

> But this misunderstanding in their reading was only possible because of a misunderstanding of Marx's object itself: a misunderstanding that made the Economists read their own object into Marx, instead of reading another object in Marx which is not their own but quite a different one. (Althusser, Balibar, Establet, Macherey, & Rancière, *Reading Capital: The Complete Edition*, 2016, p. 226)

Straying from Dislocation: Empiricism and Surplus Value

Wages are a noble scam. This is hard to see at first. We get paid to work. The work is worth a certain amount. The amount of money we get is supposed to be worth the amount our work is worth. Supposedly, there's an equal exchange between the people who buy our work (our bosses) and who sells it (us). Easy.

But think about it. The company is trying to make a profit. The employers want to make more money than it takes them to cover their costs. They want something extra. That's why they hire us. And if we didn't do the work, the company couldn't run. We provide a particularly valuable thing, the very thing that creates their profit: work. Of course there are the supplies, buildings, infrastructure...but all of this would be pointless if there weren't people to use the supplies to do the work, go to the buildings every day to do the work, or use the infrastructure to do the work. Everything stops, no profit gets made, without the people that do the work. There's something distinctive and strange about getting paid by bosses to do this work when the purpose of the work is to make the bosses a profit. We're selling our work for a fixed price, and the bosses give us that amount, but the bosses benefit when they pay us because they make a profit. What they pay us is fixed but the profit is something extra, beyond what it took to pay us. The bosses get that something extra because they own everything else. The exchange of money for work is supposed to be an equal exchange—money for work—but it isn't an equal exchange because of how important the work is to their profit.

If the work we do for the bosses was worth exactly as much as the money we get from them, the bosses would either be socialist or stupid. For the exchange to happen there has to be something in it for the bosses, they have to get something extra that we don't get. What they get in exchange for our work is the profit our work generates, which is always more than what we get paid. So our work is worth more than what they pay us for it. The employer always comes away with more than we do. At least, the point of paying us a fixed amount is to help them make the money that we will not get. That's the goal in capitalism.

People say they don't get paid enough for what they do. In a capitalist economy, that's always true no matter how much we get paid. In capitalism, if we're paid for the work we do, it's always true by definition that we don't get paid enough to do what we do. It would be absurd to pay us enough, because the point is for the bosses to make something more than what they pay us.

This something extra that we create but don't get, this money that we make for someone else, is an example of what Marx called surplus value. It's surplus because it's extra, something that workers make, since we produce it, but don't make, since we don't take it home.

Althusser writes that it's hard to measure surplus value. It's difficult to observe it unless you think about capitalism and value the way Marx did. Classical and neoclassical economists don't measure surplus value because they don't see it. For them, surplus value isn't a thing. They think about capitalism empirically, through what they observe. Being a Marxist means thinking that thinking isn't having thoughts about what you see. Instead, for Marxists, thinking means thinking about seeing what you see because you think in a certain way: that thoughts come from somewhere.

Again, empiricists disagree. They say that thinking is having thoughts about what you see, period. If you see enough things that confirm a certain thought then you can say that the thought is true. Empiricism is the first way to not follow the law of dislocation: thinking that the object of knowledge isn't a concrete-in-thought, but rather an observation-in-thought. Rather than concepts worked on through theoretical practices in parallel with the world of things, observations, according to empiricists, supposedly converge with the world of things through perception. Once empiricists perceive something enough, they claim to have found something. They claim to see evidence of the object of knowledge in the real object. For them, knowledge is both about reality and out and about in reality.

The object of knowledge, for empiricists, is located in the real object because they observe it. The real object isn't a concrete-real but rather an abstract-real where stuff happens according to laws of nature. Natural law is the essence of the phenomena, to put it one way. However you put it, empiricists locate the object of knowledge in the real object—because, perception. Thus the empiricist sees gold in the dross, naturally, and gets persnickety when questioned about that observation being true or false or whatever. Since empirical economists don't observe surplus value, for example, they don't think it's a thing. All they see are contracts for wages or salaries and money for work. They don't see exploitation, for example, because they think that thoughts are just about what they can see, not the other way around (that what they see is really about their thoughts).

The law of dislocation says that there are no natural laws, only theories constructed through some knowledge production process over time in parallel with the world of things. These theories are about reality and in parallel with reality. But what the theory says is there is never really there: the two are dislocated. Marx's contribution to political economy, Althusser says, was to see that seeing isn't what empiricists say it is. Surplus value is a paradigm case.

Petty, Laplace, and Capital Vol. 1

There were two important statisticians in the history of social science: William Petty and Pierre Simon-Laplace. Petty was a British economist. He was one of the first people to collect mortality rates for the government. He went around asking churches for the number of burials they had done each year. He thought that the numbers told their own truth, that percentages and quantities of observable phenomena based on data told certain truths. Laplace had a different approach to statistics. He studied the philosophy of Aristotle, particularly the part about causality. Like Petty, Laplace ventured out to collect data with the purpose of showing whether a certain social thing, like mortality rates, was caused by another social thing. He used Aristotle's forms of causality to articulate his conclusions. His goal was to show how these Aristotelian ideas were true or false using the data. Whereas Petty thought that concepts only came from data collection (which were just observations), Laplace thought that data was collected for the purpose of confirming or denying certain kinds of concepts.

Petty didn't follow the law of dislocation, but Laplace was on the right track. Any data collected, any measurement or observation, always happens at the service of a certain concept, which is dislocated from what it describes.

A final example: when you read Marx's magnum opus *Capital, Vol. 1*, you might be surprised and frustrated by the first chapter. It's a conceptual analysis of value, examining the idea of exchange-value and how it differs from use-value. The chapter is a conceptual intervention, not a measurement of certain quantities or the introduction of a certain set of measurements, with which some mainstream economists at that time might have started their big books. But Marx's big book isn't about what we observe in capitalist economies. It's rather about the ideas on which justifications for capitalist economies rely. The book begins with theory. It doesn't start with what we perceive and observe, but rather what we can think about about what we observe. Marx knew that you have to focus first on theories, since theories are always in parallel with reality. You have to start with the abstract, as Althusser says. Marx knew that the object of knowledge is dislocated from the real object, and he begins his magnum opus by insisting on a new object of knowledge that helps us see what is really going on with capitalism: that it's based on the noble scam of exploitation. Though Marx never articulates it, Althusser says, he expounds the law of dislocation there. Being a Marxist, for Althusser, means changing the way you think about thought and reality because that's what Marx had to do to see capitalism for what it was.

> This silent confrontation of a consciousness (living its own situation in the dialectical-tragic mode, and believing the whole world to be moved by its impulse) with a reality which is indifferent and strange to this so-called dialectic and apparently undialectical reality, makes possible an immanent critique of the illusions of consciousness...Marx's fundamental principle that it is impossible for any form of ideological consciousness to contain in itself, through its own internal dialectic, an escape from itself, that, strictly speaking, there is no dialectic of consciousness: no dialectic of consciousness which could reach reality itself by virtue of its own contradictions; in short, there can be no 'phenomenology' in the Hegelian sense: for consciousness does not accede to the real through its own internal development, but by the radical discovery of what is other than itself. (Althusser, *For Marx, The 'Piccolo Teatro': Bertolazzi and Brecht: Notes on a Materialist Theatre*, 2005d, p. 143)

Leaves, Monads, and Other Simple Internal Essences

In the Werner Herzog film *The White Diamond*, the German documentarian has a conversation with a man from an indigenous community in Guyana,

South America. At one point, Herzog sees a drop of water on a leaf. In a state of wonderment, Herzog exclaims that the whole of the universe could be contained within this one drop of water on the leaf. The indigenous man replies with a smirk, basically replying that, well, it's just a drop of water on a leaf.

In this vignette, Herzog thought that the droplet of water expressed the entirety of the universe, that a part of the universe contained the whole. This part-whole relation is sometimes called a synecdoche: when a part expresses the whole, or *pars totalis* in Latin. Mandelbrot equations, when graphed, show the same kind of pattern. The numbers of these equations produce an image where, if you zoom out to the largest scale of the graph, you see a shape that looks like a paisley pattern, a swirling paramecium-like curl. But if you pick any point on this graph and zoom in to the smallest scale of that point, you will see the same paisley pattern, the same paramecium-like shape. The small is in the large and the large is in the small.

The German philosopher G. W. Leibniz articulated a theory of monads that said roughly the same thing: that nature is made of particles that contain every other particle. Each such monad is as complex as the whole of every monad. The early French sociologist Gabriel Tarde's theory of society was based on this monadic idea, that smaller social practices contained the whole of society within them. The German poet J. W. Goethe had a similar botanical theory, claiming that each leaf of a plant contains the entirety of the plant itself. The plant is in the leaf, and in the leaf the plant.

Each of these theories puts an essence in a phenomenon: leaf, droplet, and paisley shape are the essences of the plant, universe, and graphed Mandelbrot equation. These essences are simple essences because they're clear and distinct parts of the whole, reduced and purified. A leaf is simpler than its plant. A droplet of water is simpler than the universe within which it exists. These essences are internal because they contain the whole within themselves. In other words, they're sufficient and necessary unto themselves, excluding the necessity of any other factor in their being. Althusser would call such things—or the epistemological concept behind them—simple internal essences.

Shades of Hegel

G. W. F. Hegel was a philosopher writing in 18th century Germany. To Althusser, his philosophy is one of simple internal essences, generalizing the expressive or speculative theory illustrated above to all of history and thought. Hegel (as summarized by Althusser, no reading is innocent) thought that there was such a thing as the Idea, which contains within it every other idea, and that history is the movement of ideas towards this Idea. Humans, because they're rational, have ideas, and our actions and cultures and civilizations manifest according to these ideas. We develop according to whether the ideas go toward or away from the Idea. Some cultures are advanced, which means that they have the Idea or are close to the Idea, but others are backwards because they don't have the idea (or the Idea). European civilization, for Hegel, had the Idea. In this case, the Idea is the essence of the phenomena: the civilization manifests the idea. The idea exists in a way that the thing doesn't. An idea expresses a whole culture, and the culture expresses the idea.

This theory is a second way not to follow the law of dislocation, which Althusser called Hegelian, or expressive theory: to claim that thought isn't a concrete-in-thought, but rather a real-in-thought. Thought in this case is the essence of the world of things, which are contingent phenomena that either express the Idea or don't express the Idea. Whereas empiricists locate the object of knowledge in the real object via observation, expressivists turn the object of knowledge into the real object so that thoughts are more real than things; so that the world of ideas is an essential reality of which the world of things is a phenomenon. The object of knowledge is therefore located in the real object, but in the Hegelian expressive theory thought is real and things are contingent to thought. This expressive theory, one that has simple internal essences where parts contain wholes, is what Althusser calls a circle of circles.

A person working with this expressive theory will say the gold is the essence of the dross. The gold is the Idea of the dross. The gold is a simple internal essence of dross. And because of this, they're knowledge is a circle of circles.

Expressivism: (Dig Here)

Althusser articulates a number of objections to expressivism, one of which ends with a two-word parenthetical: (dig here). The expressive theory, he says, points to one single place and directs us to dig there for the truth, to look there and only there. But the theory never actually does the looking. It says to dig in one spot, to look at something deeply, but doesn't dig. There are two critiques here. First, expressivism tells us to dig but doesn't compel us to dig, and is happy for us to remain on the surface of things. Second, once the theory tells us to dig in a particular place, the theory is stuck at that spot in particular and won't consider much else except that spot. This limitation is like the driver who has lost their keys somewhere in a parking lot at night and only looks for them underneath a street lamp, which happens to provide some light. The light is only there in that one spot, limiting the search. The expressive Hegelian theory, to Althusser, is a theory of simple internal essences which ultimately tells us to dig somewhere, to look only where the lamplight is shining, leaving the complex and difficult world of things in darkness.

Human Nature

The law of dislocation claims that the real object isn't the object of knowledge, nor is the object of knowledge the real object. Thought is parallel to reality. The world of ideas are about the world of things, but ideas are never out and about. This means that the real object is neither the object of knowledge (expressivism) nor is the object of knowledge there in the real object (empiricism).

As another example, consider a common refrain: it's just human nature. This phrase is humanism, of a kind: that human beings have a nature, humans are a certain way, humanity and humanness and mankind and human being itself all come with a concept of human essence. Althusser famously rejected humanism, and maybe now you can see why: the idea that human beings are a certain way—that persons, beings, people, you me and everyone we know—*are essentially human* doesn't follow the law of dislocation. Making this claim is another version of saying the gold is in the dross, playing the mental sleight of hand mentioned at the beginning where a concept is switched out for the reality. The concept of human being or human nature, said in that way, locates an object of knowledge in a real object. According to the law of dislocation, it doesn't make sense to talk about human nature except as an object of knowledge that comes from somewhere, a concept with a history that's parallel to the real object of human beings. We aren't essentially gendered or raced or classed or specied or sexualized, for example. Rather, all of these concretes-in-thought have been produced through knowledge processes, theoretical practices, and have come to bear on us and in us for certain reasons over time. It may be powerful and expedient to think that humans are human beings, or have races or genders. Thinking this way was a key concept in the transition between modes of production in Europe, in creating secularism from Christianity, in abolitionist causes, human rights causes and other liberation struggles. It's power and expediency may make it a correct concept under certain circumstances, but no matter how correct it will always be an object of knowledge dislocated from the real object.

In some places, Althusser keeps the two theories that disagree with the law of dislocation—empiricism and expressivism—separate, but in others he says they are related: expressivism, he says, is a kind of empiricism. It's sensuous empiricism, whereas the other perspective is a rational empiricism. But he also says these are both types of idealism, where abstractions are said to be in some meaningful way over and above concrete things, transcending the world of concrete things. Another way to think about these two theories are as essentialisms: each of them pose an essential and inessential part of reality, claiming that thought accesses the former and leaves the latter aside. Empiricists think there are natural essences that the fields of biology or chemistry or economics can uncover through observation; expressivists think there are rational essences which express in thought the totalities of which they are a part. While Marx was influenced by these idealists with their essentialisms and transcendences, he also disagreed with them. He rejected them both, says Althusser, articulating a new theory. To make that theory he had to use the tools of his forebears, but ultimately he parted ways with them. To Althusser, Marx is a materialist (not idealist), an anti-essentialist (not an essentialist), and an immanentist (not a transcendentalist).

Marxist theory is therefore a break, a rupture, and a new problematic. Althusser uses the word problematic as a noun to refer to a theory, or a schema of understanding, perhaps an ideology or science emerging in a particular historical context, that furnishes certain concepts behind words. The philosopher of science Thomas Kuhn called these paradigms, but for Althusser (and his reading of Marx) the paradigms emerge from class struggle. New findings that disrupt previously held beliefs, theoretical revolutions, discoveries, and epiphanies, these are all sometimes called paradigm shifts. Althusser, following French philosophers of science George Canguelheim and Gaston Bachelard, called such paradigms "problematics" and changes in problematics he called "epistemological breaks"—a Marxist theory of paradigm shifts.

> Understanding an ideological argument implies, at the level of the ideology itself, simultaneous, conjoint knowledge of the ideological field in which a thought emerges and grows; and the exposure of the internal unity of this thought: its problematic. Knowledge of the ideological field itself presupposes knowledge of the problematics compounded or opposed in it. This interrelation of the particular problematics of the thoughts belonging to the ideological allows of a decision as to its author's specific difference, i.e., whether a new meaning has emerged. Of course, this complex process is all haunted by real history. (Althusser, *For Marx, On the Young Marx*, 2005c, p. 70)

> A theory which enables us to see clearly in Marx, to distinguish science from ideology, to deal with the difference between them within the historical relation between them and to deal with the discontinuity of the epistemological break within the continuity of a historical process, a theory which makes it possible to distinguish a word from a concept, to distinguish the existence or non-existence of a concept behind a word, to discern the existence of a concept by a word's function in the theoretical discourse, to define the nature of a concept by its function in the problematic, and thus by the location it occupies in the system of the 'theory'; this theory which alone makes possible an authentic reading of Marx's writings, a reading which is both epistemological and historical, this theory is in fact simply Marxist philosophy itself. (Althusser, *For Marx, On the Young Marx*, 2005c, p. 39)

Concepts behind 'Words'

You might read the word object. Or the word reality. You might think that the words mean roughly the same thing when you read them in different contexts. But when it comes to theories, the same words go in front of different concepts. For example, people encountering philosophy for the first time are tempted to look up words in the dictionary to be able to say once and for all what words like reality or object or knowledge mean. Looking up words during philosophical debates is an escape from the difficulty of philosophy, however, which is the difficulty of thinking about the concepts behind words. Theories of reality and knowledge are so different that the words might as well be different, so the dictionary never helps. The struggle of ideas, the history of philosophy, is a struggle over the words' concepts. To do theoretical work, you have to understand the shifts in problematics even as the words stay in place.

When John Locke, who was an empiricist, writes the word 'real' it comes in front of an entirely different concept of reality than when Descartes, a rationalist, writes the word 'real.' The same goes for Plato and Nietzsche, or any theorist who has initiated a break from previous problematics for any load-bearing word like object, existence, knowledge, or truth. The concept behind a word is a problematic. It has a history. What theorists do is work on problematics and hammer out new ones, or articulate aspects of existing ones, or repeat old ones in new ways relevant to their moments. Theorists are always talking about which problematics are the same, which are different, and how; or which ones are new or old; or which ones lead to certain conclusions or applications. A problematic is an object of knowledge which is about (but, for Marxist theory, never out and about) the real object. The empiricist problematic claims that what is extracted from the real object via perception and abstraction is really part of the real object. The expressivist problematic imbues the object of knowledge as being the essence of the real object. The Marxist problematic breaks with the empiricist and expressivist problematics, claiming that the object of knowledge is about the real object, but never converges with it.

Althusser has a way of indicating where a problematic might be lurking behind a word, or signaling that the problematic behind a word deserves more attention. Following a practice that Vladminir Lenin used in his writing, and also many philosophers of language, Althusser frequently uses scare quotes, single apostrophes around words or phrases. Any time a word bears a load, comes in front of a problematic, or is a terrain where different forces compete to establish the concept behind the word or phrase, 'the word or phrase will get put in scare quotes just like this.' The scare quotes mean the word has competing concepts. In other words, the person who writes the word isn't innocent, nor the person reading it. They work with a problematic that arises out of their moment, experience, and their material situation.

A Theory of Reading: Listening to Silence

The law of dislocation therefore comes with a theory of reading. If the world of ideas is separate from the world of things, and theorizing means producing concretes-in-thought through other concretes-in-thought out of yet other concretes-in-thought, all of which are about the world of things but not out and about the world of things, then we have to pay close attention to the concretes-in-thought at play in any utterance. We should listen carefully to any sentence parading as knowledge: we have to read the words as always coming in front of problematics, concepts emerging from history, which will not be immediately apparent. Reading is listening to the problematics, the paradigms-in-history at play behind the words. Althusser calls this listening to the silences.

Althusser says Marx listened to the silences in Hegel (expressivism) and the classical political economists like Adam Smith and David Ricardo (empiricism). He claims that Marx worked on these concepts and produced a new problematic for his time, produced an epistemological break in problematics, hammered out a new object of knowledge that gives an unprecedented vision of the real object of society, producing both a new concept for the word 'science' and thus a new way to understand society, but also reality itself. A centerpiece of this new problematic, the concept behind the word 'reality,' is the concept of uneven development.

CHAPTER 3

The Law of Uneven Development

> We still have to learn the essential feature of this practice: the law of uneven development. For as Mao puts it in a phrase as clear as the dawn, 'Nothing in this world develops absolutely evenly.' To understand the meaning of this law and its scope—and, contrary to what is sometimes thought, it does not concern imperialism alone, but absolutely 'everything in this world'....
>
> LOUIS ALTHUSSER, *For Marx, On the Materialist Dialectic*, 2005b, p. 201

∙∙∙

> To make the matter clearer in a few words: when you reject the radical origin of things, whatever the figure used, you need to create quite different categories from the classical ones in order to get a grasp on those notions—essence, cause or liberty—whose authority is drawn from this origin. When you reject the category of origin as a philosophical issuing bank, you have to refuse its currency too, and put other categories into circulation...
>
> LOUIS ALTHUSSER, *Philosophy and the Spontaneous Philosophy of the Scientists and Other Essays, Is it Simple to be a Marxist in Philosophy?*, 1990a, p. 217

∙∙

Every Thing Is a Mess

Reality is a mess. We have ideas about the mess and sometimes those ideas compel us to act in ways that make a difference in the mess. But it's always a mess.

I taught high school in Washington, DC, for a number of years. One day an older student fell asleep in my class. While this was common with other students, she was different: typically very assiduous, focused. I perceived her falling asleep as a bad pattern, disrespectful to me and dangerous to her progress. Sleeping in class, to me, was the mark of a bad student. It was a Catholic school and I was a new teacher and colleagues had said they sometimes made students stand if they slept. I reacted hastily and angrily. I asked her to stand. She started crying.

After class I asked her why she had been sleeping and why she cried. She said her house had caught fire the previous week and her mother and sister had been living in their car, without any place to go. Many of my students lived this life of poverty. As a middle-class person I didn't know what that was like but I was learning, slowly. I was shocked, saddened, ashamed. I apologized. I asked what I could do.

I use this anecdote to remember that reality is a structured mess, a welter of patterned tensions pressuring any given object in multiple ways that overflow my knowledge of them. As a teacher I try to prevent the tendency of thinking that any object of knowledge I produce about my students' lives ever converges with the real object of my students' lives. Their lives, the lives of others, of reality itself, is a balance of forces where some forces are dominant over others, creating tensions and torsions and contradictions that perhaps even the others themselves don't fully understand. I refuse to essentialize my students, or idealize them, or idealize their circumstances.

The real object—any given real object, small or large—is always in a state of structured mess. Time passes and the mess shifts in particular ways under particular circumstances. History layers itself. Forces pressure other forces; they win and lose; they're frustrated and fulfilled. There's no law that can predict or describe the movements in general, though there are ways to understand their contours and make a difference in them; to understand some of the variations and their structure and intervene. Some people are better at charting the contours of forces to intervene in them than others. There's a law that has language for describing the structured mess, to chart the contours of forces and change them more intentionally: the law of uneven development. This law has concepts that we can use to talk about the structured mess of reality, how it forms, stays the same, and changes. This law of uneven development follows from the law of dislocation and is one of Althusser's major contributions (though he would claim it's Marx's contribution) to intellectual history.

Lenin understood uneven development. Althusser writes that Lenin could find the weakest link in the chain of a political reality and figure out a way to break it. 'Weakest link in the chain' has a concept behind it, and that concept is the law of uneven development, or the way that forces gather into structured pressure points under particular circumstances. Antonio Gramsci understood this as well: when he first translated Marx into Italian he inserted the word terrain into the phrasing of class struggle, so that it read "the terrain of class struggle" in Italian. He knew that society was an undulating set of forces, elements acting on one another in different directions in different ways. The word terrain indicates the concept of uneven development. In Gramsci's theory, groups win hegemony by exerting forces to become dominant in the structured variations of a social formation.

Remember that dross stands for the real object in Althusser's metaphor. Think about dross: sedimentary layers, un-mined and un-panned. There are staggered lines between layers of differently-colored rock, particles, sand, and grains (like those depicted on the cover of this book). Each layer is there, present, structured. Each exerts a force and each grain composing its layer exerts a force and is exerted upon. Every region of the dross has a particular set of circumstances in relation to the other regions and each particle bears this relation to every other particle. Water runs around it. Air passes through it, heats, and cools it. Gravity, the sheer force of matter, acts on it and in it. Beings traverse it, live and die and defecate and reproduce on it. The dross changes. It's structured, but the structure is a confluence of variations particular to it and its moment. Reality, in Althusser's theory, is structured like sedimentary layers of rock. Like a terrain. Some variations are preponderant, major, or in excess, while other variations are under-formed, absent, minor. Major forces dominate, minor forces are kept subordinate. There are threads of gold, yes, but threads of so many other elements as well, each of which relate to one another and exert forces both individually as elements and as elements in variation with one another (and variations relating to one another beyond that). A structured mess in dominance.

To think that the gold is some real object, some essence—to think that there is any essence there in the dross—doesn't follow the law of dislocation, and also doesn't follow the law of uneven development. To appreciate the dross as the real object and conceive of the object of knowledge as an extraction process occurring within and on structured variations, structured in dominance; to always see patterned unevenness in the changes of things: that's thinking with the law of uneven development.

> Hegel thought of society as a *totality*, while Marx thought of it as a complex whole, structured in dominance. If I may be allowed to be a little provocative, it seems to me that we can leave to Hegel the category of *totality*, and claim for Marx the category of the *whole*. It might be said that this is a verbal quibble, but I do not think this is entirely true. If I preferred to reserve for Marx the category of the whole rather than that of the totality, it is because within the totality a double temptation is always present: that of considering it as a pervasive essence which exhaustively embraces all of its manifestations, and—what amounts to the same thing—that of discovering in it, as in a circle or a sphere (a metaphor which makes us think of Hegel once again), a center which would be its essence. (Althusser, *Philosophy and the Spontaneous Philosophy of the Scientists and Other Essays*, 1990, p. 219)

The DSA

As an example of how this concept can be put to use, consider the following. I'm a member of the Democratic Socialists of America. This organization has haphazardly become a hope of the Left in the United States. We had a national convention in 2017 where delegates elected leadership. The election was a competition between 43 individuals for 16 spots. Some of these individuals—some of the best organized—ran as slates. The slates had platforms: strategies for what the DSA should and shouldn't do.

One slate called itself Momentum after the organization that brought the English politician Jeremy Corbyn to power. Momentum's platform included a somewhat idealized view of the labor movement. By encouraging and growing progressive caucuses that push for democratic unions, they said, the DSA should rebuild the labor movement to become the fighting force for the working class that it should be. The labor movement, for them, should become like the Chicago Teachers Union strike in Chicago, the Working Educators caucus in Philadelphia, Teamsters for a Democratic Union, and others. Yet these groups aren't representative of the labor movement in the United States. Labor is a mess. This mess is striated with threads of tensions throughout many sectors, each of which depend and don't depend on one another in particular ways. Industrial, manufacturing, and service sectors face unique challenges and move at differential rates. The organization and movement of the working class has a racial and gendered character, glass walls and ceilings everywhere. Threats from right to work legislation abound: our country is a right to work country. Barely 11% of workers are unionized. The reality of labor is a structured mess.

An analysis, a scientific one, would have looked at this mess and found a weak link in the chain, a place to push, a way to intervene that took into account the balance of forces at work in the labor movement. But it didn't. It chose a thread of gold in the dross, claimed it as an essence, and sold it during the leadership campaign. Of course it was a good idea (ideally, the labor movement should be stronger and more oriented towards class struggle and socialism), but it wasn't necessarily correct since, materially, the labor movement is extremely uneven. The strategy didn't take this unevenness into account.

On the other hand, the Momentum slate advocated fighting for single-payer healthcare as a flagship campaign. This has the makings of a correct decision. The ground is ripe for a new healthcare system in the United States, both centrist and conservative plans haven't worked. There's an opening in the balance of forces. Not only that but it could be a shift that makes a difference at the site of a tension in that balance of forces, since—as the slate said—healthcare ties workers to their employers. With healthcare provided for free at the point of service independently of employment, workers are freed up to do other things, not to mention live a healthy life. This would be a serious jab, if not an uppercut, to the dominant relations of production, the relations of wage work and exploitation. It would be more difficult to exploit workers at will if they had healthcare taken care of by the government. In the United States conjuncture, considered as a structured whole, such a shift could make a decisive difference. The decision to focus on this campaign was both a good idea and a correct idea given the balance of forces in the country since it took into account the terrain and its uneven undulations, and suggested an intervention with the potential to make a decisive shift in that balance. Healthcare is a weak link in the chain of American capitalism and breaking that link, already stretched too tightly, could loosen the entire chain.

In this case, Momentum's labor strategy was essentializing whereas its healthcare strategy wasn't, since the former thought of labor in terms of a simple internal essence of progressive caucuses and the latter considered the uneven and structured whole of the US social formation and recommended an intervention that could shift it.

Theory of Combination

The law of uneven development has a set of theoretical terms that we should define and theories to elaborate. A variation is an arrangement of elements and relations. It's a combine with articulated parts, like a body with limbs. By the fact of its particular presence, a variation can exert force and can be exerted upon by the forces emerging from other variations, or combinations of variations. Since no two entities can occupy the same space and between any two entities is a relation, entities pressure others. The force a variation exerts might be incommensurate with its size or extent. Variations combine to form other variations. Entities and relations form up in variations, and variations emerge within variations, all of which exert forces. Large combinations of variations are regions. Thinking of the real object as being composed of entities related to one another in variations which exert force is the theory of combination.

When variations combine they pressure one another and shift, moving into a balance with one another. Things stay in place because variations array themselves stably, remaining in a formation in dominance, where certain variations dominate. Yet there are always torsions, tensions, mutations, fractures, splits, staggerings. There are condensations, residues, survivals. There are ruptures, explosions, and breaks. There are encounters. There's reproduction of the existing balance of forces over time (maintenance, continuity) and revolutions when that balance breaks and gives way to another balance. Each of these terms like break, torsion, split and others is a kind of movement in the balance of forces, which the variations form as they combine.

Theory of Formation

This theory of combination implies another theory of formation, which says that that the real object (any thing) is a formation of structured variations in dominance. Society, for instance, according to this theory, is a social formation: a balance of social forces exerted by combines of social entities, relations, and variations where some of those variations dominate.

The status of any entity or relation or variation, or any region formed by variations, the status of their ability to move in any given way, is always relative to the specific balance of forces they exist within. There will be always exceptional circumstances, particular pressures exerted by variations near and far in the balance, which permit, don't permit, or don't not permit certain kinds of action. Their degrees of freedom are relative to the balance of forces. The extent to which they can and do move independently is always nonzero (there is freedom) but this independent movement is always relative to their position in their specific balance of forces. The extent to which each entity, with its relations and variations and location in the balance of forces, can move according to a variation of its "own making"—the extent an entity or variation can swerve, to use a term from Lucretius—is relative to its position in the formation.

Theory of Relative Autonomy

The theories of combination and formation imply a theory of relative autonomy. Each entity, relation, variation, and region is relatively autonomous: it can swerve in an independent way but always relative to the balance of forces it exists within, which means that this swerving depends to some extent on that balance. The theory of relative autonomy is a theory of indexed effectivity: the balance of forces determines the extent to which entities and variations within it can swerve, while the entities and variations themselves constitute the balance of forces. The extent to which particular variations can determine their own movement within the structured whole of their formation (relative autonomy) provides an index of the structured whole's effectivity, as well as an index of the particular variation's effectivity.

Theory of Determination

So we get a theory of determination too: any particular variation both determines and is determined by the balance of forces, such that its movement is always relatively autonomous given the index of effectivity of that balance of forces. Any part of the balance of forces, any variation or region, has a determinate location in the formation which—depending on the extent to which the variation can move autonomously—provides an index of effectivity. Determination occurs through the relatively autonomous movement of variations in the balance of forces. Swerving and emerging forces exert pressures on one another and the structured whole. But changes in the balance of forces don't happen through simple determination of one variation or region on another: there is overdetermination when there's an excess of forces acting on a region or variation, and underdetermination when there is a dearth of such force. Althusser borrowed this term overdetermination from psychoanalysis to talk about the plural character of causal forces in a social formation. Effects are over- or under-determined, but rarely (if ever) simply determined.

According to these theories of combination, formation, relative autonomy, and determination the balance of forces is uneven. A mess. Society, as a social formation, is what Antonio Gramsci called a terrain. Variation, combination, balance of forces, formation, movement, relative autonomy, effectivity, determination: dross.

Variations move and determine and are determined by one another through forces they exert. The formation develops. "Time" is the rate of change in each determinant location of the balance of forces, though each variation moves differentially at its own pace. There are many rates of change, some quick and others slow. Some almost inert and others roiling. The balance of forces unevenly develops according these differential times. This concept of uneven development, the changes structured variations make within a formation of combinations, is Althusser's concept of dialectics and history.

> As a first approximation, we can argue from the specific structure of the Marxist whole that it is no longer possible to think the process of development of the different levels of the whole *in the same historical time*. Each of these different 'levels' does not have the same type of historical existence. On the contrary, we have to assign to each level a *peculiar time*, relatively autonomous and hence relatively independent, even in its dependence, of the 'times' of the other levels. We can and must say: for each mode of production there is a peculiar time and history, punctuated

> in a specific way by the development of the productive forces; the relations of production have their peculiar time and history, punctuated in a specific way; the political superstructure has its own history...; philosophy has its own time and history...; aesthetic productions have their own time and history...; scientific formations have their own time and history, etc. Each of these peculiar histories is punctuated with peculiar rhythms and can only be known on condition that we have defined the *concept* of the specificity of its historical temporality and its punctuations (continuous development, revolutions, breaks, etc.). The fact that each of these times and each of these histories is *relatively autonomous* does not make them so many domains which are *independent* of the whole: the specificity of each of these times and of each of these histories—in other words, their relative autonomy and independence—is based on a certain type of articulation in the whole, and therefore on certain type of dependence with respect to the whole...The specificity of these times and histories is therefore *differential*, since it is based on the differential relations between the different levels within the whole: the mode and degree of *independence* of each time and history is therefore necessarily determined by the mode and degree of *dependence* of each level within the set of articulations of the whole. (Althusser, Balibar, Establet, Macherey, & Rancière, *Reading Capital: The Complete Edition*, 2016, p. 247)

The Wrong Side of History

If a change in the real object, which develops unevenly, is always the result of a set of forces working on a total balance of forces, then there is no one single time. There are always many times, a time for each region, each variation. There will be no Rate of Change that is the ultimate rate of change across the entire real object. Rather, there are only rates of change. Applying this idea to history yields some unsettling consequences.

When Barack Obama took office and officially became President of the United States in 2009, his inaugural speech had a phrase that he would utter throughout this eight years as president: the wrong side of history. He said that his election marked the line between those who are on the wrong side of history and those who aren't. History, in this ideology, proceeds according to a political progression where the present moment is the best it has ever been, the moments before the present have been less good, and the moments after this moment will be even better than now. Events proceed on this single straight line into a glorious future...so long as we don't misstep to the wrong side.

I remember those hopeful days with bitterness now. I recall the power of those particular words, the wrong side of history, coming from the first Black president of a country whose original sin is African slavery. I remember the phrase getting stuck in my teeth, though. Wrong side of history. I thought about its implication: the right side of history. Who is on the right side of history, and how do we know? Does history have sides? What are those sides? I didn't make too much of it then, but now these questions have more intense meaning. As I write this book, the liberal-democratic institutions Obama advocated and in which he invested so much are crumbling under the weight of an imperial capitalism that he helped perpetuate and even grow. The erosion of these institutions, via absurdly high military spending and unrestrained financial markets, have brought us the presidency of Donald Trump. This Trump presidency is an effect in history, a change in the balance of forces of the US social formation. According to Obama's concept, what side of history are we on now? Obama was right, maybe, that history has sides like a tectonic plate. He was right also that these plates are in tension with one another, that variations of entities and their relations compound and combine in friction and torsion with one another. He was wrong however that there are only right and wrong sides of these variations and their changes over time. He may have been wrong if he thought we were on some singular "right" side of history when he took office. His election, unique though it was in the balance of forces, was just one set of variations occurring within a larger formation of other combined variations. To imply, as he did frequently, that our "greatest days" were ahead of us, ignored how history moves unevenly.

It could be that the history of race relations in the United States shifted in the balance of forces when Obama was elected, for example. But there's never one time in society: there are many times. Oscar Grant, an unarmed Black man, was murdered by police in San Francisco the night Obama was elected, and Black Lives Matter—whose primary target was police brutality—formed within the same balance of forces that elected Obama. Not to mention all the other variations present in the US social formation when Obama took office: the extent to which his presidency did and didn't shift the class struggle in the US, the gender struggle, or the colonial struggle, or any other set of forces and variations in the social formation. All of this is unclear, but we can know for sure that it's uneven. Obama deported more immigrants than any president. The criminals who caused the financial crisis in 2007–2008 walked free, received bonuses. The United States continued to incarcerate more people than any country on Earth, a disproportionate number of them Black men. War continued. Trade deals continued sucking the working class dry. Police continued killing innocents. The Democratic Party lost thousands of seats in federal, state, and local governments. Donald Trump, the man who waged the Birther campaign against Obama, was elected to succeed him. History doesn't move in a single line from wrong to right. It's relentlessly uneven. Race relations are a relatively autonomous seam of ideologies in the larger formation, affecting various regions in uneven ways. The shift in race relations may not have had a high index of effectivity on the social formation as a whole. To think that history is subject to one single force, one variation—that there's a right and wrong side, and the past is wrong and the future right—is a common empiricist, idealist mistake. Another gold-dross sleight of hand. According to the law of uneven development, there's no wrong side of history, just an uneven structure in dominance, a social formation of precariously balanced variations moving at differential paces, each with differential effectivities within the larger balance of their forces.

Acorns

For a very different example of how the law of uneven development changes the concept of time, take acorns. You might say that an acorn contains the oak tree, or that the seed carries the plant within it. Within the beginning is the end, as T.S. Eliot wrote. Development in this case is evenly rolled up inside the acorn and unfurls in an inevitable way along a path. Hegel used this acorn metaphor. Althusser disagreed. Instead, particular acorns go through particular stages of development at particular times and places. Oak tree growth is uneven. Some acorns never take root. Some oak trees die young. Others deform or mutate. Some are eaten, chopped down, burned, or get diseases. No single acorn contains an oak tree, but some acorns do grow into certain kinds of oak trees that lead certain kinds of lives under certain conditions. In reality, according to the law of uneven development, the lives of acorns are uneven.

Teleology on the Train

As another example of the law of uneven development, take the philosophical word "teleology." *Telos* is Greek for end, or aim. If you think that the oak tree is in the acorn then you have a teleological theory of acorns, because the acorn has its end goal in the oak tree: the acorn essentially proceeds towards the oak tree. Like Obama, if you think the present moment is the best it has ever been, the past has been less good, and the future will be better, you have a teleological theory of progress: history proceeds from better to worse. While teleological theories are appealing, and even appear true in some cases, they don't take unevenness into account. In the case of acorns, an acorn might

THE LAW OF UNEVEN DEVELOPMENT 47

never take root, or a sapling oak could die from a fire. In the case of American history, Donald Trump could get elected president and succeed Barack Obama.

Another good example comes from public transportation. Taking the train to your destination isn't the same as going to the train's ultimate destination. I used to live in New York City and took the subway everywhere. Each subway line went in a particular direction. When I first lived in New York City, I would commute to Columbia University from Bergen Street in Brooklyn. I took the 2 or 3 train going north, where I would get off at 96th street, switch to the 1 train and then arrive at 116th street. When I got on the 2 train at Bergen Street, that train was headed toward Harlem-148th street. I would step on the train and the electronic announcement system would say "this is the train to Harlem-148th street." Making teleological claims about history or acorns or any development would be like claiming that my ultimate destination was Harlem-148th street, even though I was getting off at 96th and switching trains. Just because the train ultimately goes somewhere doesn't mean that anyone who gets on that train is ultimately going to that place. Instead, different people go radically different places on the same train. Certainly some riders go to the train's final destination, but it's probably only a small percentage of anyone riding the train at a given moment (and, if we're being specific, that train reverses and ultimately goes back and forth along that track). The real object of train ridership is uneven. The essence of the 2 or 3 train isn't its ultimate destination at Harlem-148th, like expressivists would say. And just because an empiricist steps onto this train and observes that the train is ultimately going to Harlem-148th street, that doesn't mean that everyone on the train is really going there. Reality is much more uneven.

> Here again we also find forms of temporality that do not achieve any mutual integration, which have no relation to one another, which coexist and interconnect, but never meet each other, so to speak; with lived elements which interlace in a dialectic which is localized, separate, and apparently ungrounded; works marked by an internal dissociation, an unresolved alterity. (Althusser, *For Marx, The 'Piccolo Teatro': Bertolazzi and Brecht: Notes on a Materialist Theatre*, 2005d, p. 142)

> Overdetermination designates the following essential quality of contradiction: the reflection in contradiction itself of its conditions of existence, that is, of its situation in the structure in dominance of the complex whole. (Althusser, *For Marx, On the Materialist Dialectic*, 2005b, p. 209)

Concepts of Structure: Captain Planet vs. Voltron

The law of uneven development—with its theories of combination, relative autonomy, formation, and determination—is the concept behind the word "structure" when Althusser writes it. The word structure with the law of uneven development behind it has a distinctive concept, which is very different from other concepts of structure. One way I've found to explain this distinctive concept is by contrasting two cartoons from my youth.

When I was a kid I watched a cartoon show on television called *Captain Planet*. The show had a clear political agenda: environmentalism. The bad guys included pig-faced corporate polluters who would exploit natural resources at any cost, ruining whole ecological systems. The good guys were a group of five teenagers from different parts of the world: North and South America, Africa, Asia, Europe. The teenagers were called Planeteers, since they were charged with defeating the polluters and saving the planet. They were led by a beautiful woman named Gaia, who gave each of the planeteers a ring which let them command an elemental force of nature: earth, fire, wind, water, and heart. With their rings, they could summon earthquakes, create tornadoes, and create empathy. The Planeteers worked as a team and took advice from Gaia and fought against the polluters, but there was something special they could do with their rings. If the Planeteers were in trouble, they could combine their powers and call into being a humanoid superhero called Captain Planet.

Captain Planet had masculine features, crystal skin, green hair, and could do a number of standard superhero-type things: fly, use incredible strength, etc. Captain Planet was more powerful than any of the Planeteers—he could save them if they were in trouble—but the Planeteers were the ones who brought him into being. Without them, he couldn't exist, but once he was brought into existence he was more powerful than any of the Planeteers who had called him into being. To bring Captain Planet into being, the planeteers raised their fists in the air, lifting up their rings and calling out their respective elemental powers. When Captain Planet whirled into existence out of the ether, he would say: "by your powers combined, I am Captain Planet!"

The Planeteers combined their forces and Captain Planet emerged, more powerful than any of them, resembling them but greater than them. He was ultimately dependent on his creators since they had to summon him, but once summoned he was independent. The Planeteers depended on him a lot of the time: they relied on him, they believed in him, and suffered greatly when he suffered. Captain Planet had his own personality as well. He was like a man: arms, legs, face, voice. He could fly. Captain Planet transcended the Planeteers. He was their ideal hero.

These words transcendent and ideal are sometimes used to think about structure when it comes to society, or social structure. When people say structure or structuralist they usually mean a theory that says social structure exists over and above the particular individuals and groups that create it. Social structure is can sometimes thought of as a transcendent object like Captain Planet is to the Planeteers. Again, there are always concepts behind words. The same goes for structure. Does every utterance of the word structure mean that the concept behind that word is a transcendent concept? No, because there are other concepts of structure. And other cartoons.

Voltron was another cartoon show on television I grew up watching. In this cartoon, human astronauts drove jaguar-shaped vehicles that could form together to create a single robot warrior, Voltron. Like the Planeteers, the Voltron characters combined to create their hero. But unlike Captain Planet, Voltron's actions were subject to the drivers' decisions and coordination. Voltron's actions, which were more powerful than any of the drivers on their own, were the articulated relations between the drivers and their machines. Voltron had no personality other than what the drivers created emergently among them. If one of the drivers couldn't drive, then a leg or arm would cease to function. Voltron was immanent in the drivers' coordinated decisions.

Voltron and Captain Planet are both superheroes, but their concepts are very different. One is a magical being that comes out of an ether, has his own personality and will, and can act independently of those who bring him about. The other is a machine, built by beings and operated by beings, and whose personality, will, and actions are subject to his drivers' decisions. Voltron's will is immanent rather than transcendant because its will emerges in the moment based on the actions of its parts. Voltron, as a hero, only exists in the effects of his multiple drivers. Certainly he's more powerful than any one driver, but he's only as powerful as the drivers themselves as they work together. It's actually strange to say Voltron does this or that action, wants this or that thing, because Voltron's actions and desires are immanent combinations of multiple and complex arrangements made between its drivers. There's something absent in the name Voltron, something missing, something that Captain Planet has: a singular soul, personality, will, essence. Voltron is an immanent hero and Captain Planet is a transcendent hero.

The difference between Voltron and Captain Planet is analogous to the difference between immanent structure and transcendent structure. Immanent structure is only present in the effects of a complex system that composes it, and emerges as a unity-as-whole in those effects without an essence. Transcendent structure, on the other hand, is present in its own effects. It's a unity-as-totality with a singular essence over and above its constituent parts.

Like Captain Planet, transcendent structure is a singular cause, a simple totality very much present in its effects. Transcendent structure has an evenness, a direction that it takes of its own accord: God, spirit, collective consciousness, or the society that wants and acts, for example. There's a there there in transcendant structure. Whereas for immanent structure, there are only theres there. Althusser would go on to say that Voltron is the absent cause of his actions, which are orchestrated in the theater of his drivers' collective actions. Of course Voltron is a hero, but an absent hero since Voltron's actions are the emergent decisions of its many drivers. Captain Planet is the present cause of his own actions in the singular autonomy of his will. Voltron is to immanent structure as Captain Planet is to transcendent structure.

According to the law of uneven development, a change in the real object occurs when a set of variations exert a force on the total balance of forces such that that set becomes dominant: the balance of forces is a structure in dominance. But that structure, for Althusser, is an immanent structure. Entities in their variations (like the drivers in their vehicles that form Voltron) are the elements of the structure. The variations are the combinations of plans and decisions the drivers make. Voltron as a hero, its actions, are the emergent effects of the drivers' coordinations. An immanent social structure is the whole that emerges in the effects of that social structure, an absent cause is only present in these effects.

This concept of structure isn't poststructural. Immanent structure is still structure. There's still a real object. There are changes in that object. We can have knowledge about those changes and the knowledge can be true or false or otherwise. However, the real object is never identical to the object of knowledge, and changes in the real object occur as a result of multiple forces in an immanent structure in dominance. The variations and forces combine in the structure and they are relatively autonomous. When things happen, when changes occur, each change is an effect of multiple causes: the change is overdetermined or underdetermined.

The Two Laws: Three Reflections

To end this section, let's think about the two laws—dislocation and uneven development—together. First, if you believe the law of dislocation, you believe that the object of knowledge is never located in the real object but is rather about the real object in parallel with it. But if you believe law of uneven development you will make claims about the real object. So it seems like you're saying that unevenness is really there, located in the real object. It seems like the law of uneven development contradicts the law of dislocation, and that Althusserian theory is inconsistent.

But the whole theory, the two laws taken together, is just that: in the world of ideas, about the world of things. Althusserian theory is theory after all, and we should therefore think of uneven development as being an object of knowledge that is about the real object. It's not contradictory or inconsistent to claim that objects of knowledge are dislocated from one another and then claim that, if you believe in dislocation, then your thoughts about the real object will report that the real object is uneven. They go hand in hand. Likewise, if you think that objects of knowledge are located in the real object you'll probably not think of the real object as uneven, because you'll see singular forces acting on singular forces and find evidence of some kind of transcendent structure, rather than a set of differentiated forces acting on a balance of forces to create a structure in dominance. Theories are only ever in the world of ideas and it isn't contradictory to make claims about the world of things with ideas, since that is exactly what ideas are. Althusserian theory is just another theory.

Second, Althusser will claim in parts of his writing that if you take the concepts of dislocation and uneven development seriously, you're being scientific. Sometimes he says you are being ideological if you don't. This appears polemical and accusatory, and sort of hypocritical: can Althusser claim his knowledge production process is scientific while others' are ideological? There are concepts behind words. The word science is no exception. These laws imply a concept of science and ideology. In some of Althusser's earlier writing, the term ideology as a technical term tends to mean a received opinion or common sense, or Generality I. Turning common sense into knowledge is what science does, and defending received wisdoms or common sense against positions produced through a knowledge production process is ideological. Certainly Althusser's concept of science—the knowledge production process implied by the two laws, the sweet science of struggle—is a different concept of science. His concepts of science and ideology are very different from ideas about science and ideology prevalent now. Althusser's concept of science is a sweet science born of class struggle, oriented towards producing knowledge about how and when to intervene in a balance of forces where certain sets of forces are dominant.

Finally, in practice, it's difficult to subscribe to these two laws. To remember that the real object isn't the object of knowledge and that development of the real object is uneven goes against intuition. It takes time. It requires incredulity towards accepted notions. It requires subtlety. One way of thinking about it is to remain "open." But as someone on the left politically, as someone in education, as someone in the humanities, I constantly hear that people should be open. Some philosophies are just explanations of what it means to be open rather than closed. Open and closed are metaphors. Althusserian theory is an explanation of what it means to be open: to never think that what you know is the final answer, to remember that the world is more complex than the ideas you have about it, and also remember that things are a mess structured in dominance. What distinguishes the theory from other theories is that it fights for openness. Part of being open, or, as Althusser writes, finding openings in the closures of thought, means fighting constantly against essentialism. This fight is a material fight. It's skeptical, but the position isn't skepticism. It's not idealism, but it deals with ideas. Rather, Althusser's position—summarized by dislocation and uneven development—is a fighting realism.

This fighting realism is a theory of forces becoming major and minor in an undulating balance of forces. Althusser writes with geological and chemical terms. Forces are in tension with one another. There are torsions between them, they leave residues and residuals in the wake of their changes, shifting. They mutate. Layerings and sedimentary lines form, which stagger. There are ruptures and explosions, frictions. Sometimes words from logic appear, which is a legacy of Marx's writing: there are contradictions in this balance of forces, consistencies and inconsistencies. Gramsci uses military language: battles between forces, victory of one force over another. Forces are deployed, launched. Sometimes gaming language appears: forces compete with one another in the balance to win for their side. Recently we have seen computer language appear to talk about the balance of forces in real objects: there are networks and nodes and interfaces, people plugging into projects.

The law of uneven development could potentially be used for any real object, generating scientific knowledge of any set of variations combining to form regions or immanent structures. Every thing is a mess. But the law of uneven development was generated initially from reflections on society, politics, economy: the real object of what happens when humans get together. I would argue the two laws combined, the law of dislocation and the law of uneven development, are best suited to scientific knowledge about society, or the science of history, which examines social formations, their balances of forces, and how to intervene in those balances to shift the structure in dominance.

CHAPTER 4

Theory of Social Formations

> ...the whole of Marxist revolutionary experience shows that, if the general contradiction (it has already been specified: the contradiction between the forces of production and the relations of production, essentially embodied in the contradiction between two antagonistic classes) is sufficient to define the situation when revolution is the 'task of the day,' it cannot of its own simple, direct power induce a 'revolutionary situation,' nor a fortiori a situation of revolutionary rupture and the triumph of the revolution. If this contradiction is to become 'active' in the strongest sense to become a ruptural principle, there must be an accumulation of 'circumstances' and 'currents' so that whatever their origin and sense (and many of them will necessarily be paradoxically foreign to the revolution in origin and sense, or even its 'direct opponents'), they 'fuse' into a ruptural unity: when they produce the result of the immense majority of the popular masses grouped in an assault on a regime which its ruling classes are unable to defend. Such a situation presupposes not only the 'fusion' of two basic conditions into a 'single national crisis,' but each condition considered (abstractly) by itself presupposes a 'fusion' of an 'accumulation' of contradictions.
>
> LOUIS ALTHUSSER, *For Marx, Contradiction and Overdetermination*, 2005a, p. 99

∴

Geology as Analogy for Society

Forces wend through dross. Gravity drags the sediment down to the Earth through its overwhelming mass. The dross rests on soil and rock, subject to tectonic shifts by huge plates beneath it. Friction and pressure act on each grain by and through and with other grains, which bear the weight generated collectively by regions of differently-formed sediments and rocks. Magma roils beneath everything, churning out new levels of rock from itself and the planet's core. In this formation there are balances, accumulations, and ruptures.

These geological terms provide an analogy for the theory of social formations consistent with the laws of dislocation and uneven development laid out in previous chapters. Social formations are a terrain where forces meet and settle in a balance that's always ready to shift. Variations of elements in relation with one another exert forces in the balance. These crystallize into levels, regions, and instances which pressure one another and form a whole—the social structure—the real object of society. Each element bears the structure both in terms of giving birth to force and shouldering force, and that immanent structure that emerges, like Voltron, is absent except in its effects. The variations are continuous or discontinuous: they change or stay the same. The variations also tend towards certain kinds of changes depending on their formation in the structure. The theory of social formations is therefore a theory of forces, elements, and their variations, for which Althusser developed a specific vocabulary.

Forces, Elements, and Variations in Society: Overview

According to Althusser's reading of Marx—the laws of dislocation and uneven development—there are three forces in a social formation:
- Production
- Reproduction
- Repression

There are elements that compose these forces:
- Individuals
- Subjects
- Relations

Variations of these elements form larger regions, which include:
- Economic
- Ideological (state)
- Political (state)

There are two kinds of variation in the regions of a social formation:
- Modes of production
- Apparatuses

(While it isn't in Althusser's writings, there should be be a fourth force added to this chart: a force exerted by non-human variations of elements which form non-built environments, or ecologies. This fourth force is an ecological force and needs more elaboration in the theory.)

We can think about these terms of Althusser's theory of social formations in the following way:

In general, variations of elements in relation to one another exert different kinds of forces with and against one another and emerge as regions in the social formation. Let's go into each of these in more detail, starting with the regions and working our way down.

TABLE 4.1 Theory of social formations

Social force	Region	Variations	Elements
Production	Economic	Modes of production	Relations of production, means of production, exploited workers, exploiting firms
Reproduction	Ideological	Ideological state apparatuses	School, church, family, media, sports, art, culture…
Repression	Political	Repressive state apparatus	Government, police, court system, policy, military, prisons

Economic Region

Modes of production form an economic region. Modes of production are arrangements between humans and non-humans made to tackle nature and make life together by extracting, making, distributing, consuming, and circulating objects of value. Relations of production are ways that humans relate to one another and the world around them. Means of production are the material stuff needed to make our lives together: raw materials, land, natural resources, infrastructure, labor power.

Relations of production are relationships between humans and non-humans. They are ways humans and non-humans relate to one another as they produce. They are practices that give a mode of production its distinct character, tendencies, and internal limits. Relations are therefore recognitive and distributive practices, to use Nancy Fraser's distinction. These practices recognize the consciousness of others in specific ways and provide for access to resources in specific ways. The practices that compose relations of production set up internal limits to recognition and resource access.

According to the law of uneven development, the economic region has many modes of production, but one relation of production will be dominant in the modes of production at any given time. Capitalism is an economy where exploitative relations of production dominate the modes of production: non-human and human elements arrange into relations of possession and profit. Subjects relate to one another via work, dispossession, accumulation, and exchange through markets. Wages, for instance, are a central piece of capitalist relations of production. There are different variations of these capitalist relations of production that have emerged over time: handicraft, manufacturing, industrial, financial. But there are always other subordinate modes of production within the economic region: cooperativism, barter/exchange, subsistence, socialism, communism. But in a capitalist economy where people work for money and the means of production are owned by a few who exploit the rest, the capitalist relations of production dominate over these lesser relations.

This economic region forms and is formed by a bottom-up force, a base-force without which the social formation could not sustain itself at all.

Ideological Region

An economy can't be self-standing. It needs to be taught, learned, and maintained. As new generations of people come into the world, they need to know how to get with the program: not to steal, to work for money, to get a job. Relations of production are ways of relating to other people and the world, and we're not born knowing how to relate to one another economically. Nor do we always understand how to go all by ourselves and get with the program, even as adults who have supposedly learned to get with that program. We need upbringing and reminders. There have to be ways of making that intervention to maintain and reproduce the relations of production over time. Apparatuses are these ways of intervening, propagating the requisite ideologies that maintain the integrity of the structure in dominance. Ideology is imagined relation to real conditions of existence, and these apparatuses intervene to reproduce the requisite imaginaries for a social formation's structural integrity.

The ideological region, emerging from reproductive forces exerted by certain elements in variations, is a sprawling, messy, and non-uniform ensemble of apparatuses that, through practices and gestures and movements, teach people to get with the program and remind people about how to be in the program.

People live their everyday lives in the ideological region of social formations. They create and participate in what's called culture. Cultural practices have effects, whether intended or unintended. For Althusser, culture is an ideological region of the social formation because—whether people mean to or not—cultural practices teach and maintain programs (not only dominant programs but subordinate and subaltern programs as well). Since cultural practices teach and maintain programs, they take place in apparatuses: they have a purpose and make interventions in the social formation.

Raising a family, going to church, going to school, going to the football game, listening to music, watching television (and all the fine-grained habits, movements, and gestures involved therein): all of these cultural practices teach and maintain imagined relations to real conditions of existence. These imagined relations need not be dominant relations. They could be counter-cultural families, insurgent churches, resistance schools, and revolutionary music. Yet each of these variations of elements still take place in the arena of apparatuses (family, church, school, music) that make interventions to reproduce imaginary relations to real conditions. Rather than dominant relations, these insurgent apparatuses reproduce subordinate relations—and can even be leveraged in the terrain to reduce their subordinate status and make gains towards winning hegemony for a subordinate class. Yet, by the fact of their dominance, the dominant imagined relations to real conditions get reproduced as well.

Like any thing else, ideological variations are uneven and relatively autonomous in the social formation. The ideological region is rife with conflict, contradiction, and inconsistency. As an ensemble, this region can give a social formation its lived idiosyncrasy. The ideological force is a maintenance and reproductive force, helping to make sure everyone knows how to get with the various programs in the social formation.

Culture and Agency

Freedom is an inherent quality of any social formation where forces move with and against one another, where elements in their variations struggle against and with one another. Relative autonomy is a kind of autonomy, after all. But there's no human spirit or soul or essence that guarantees freedom. Rather, freedom is a freedom in struggle and contingency in the social formation itself. Agency, or the ability of subjects like you or me to maneuver within a social formation, is also a property of the structure and not subjects themselves. Subjects, like anything else in a social formation, are relatively autonomous. Culture isn't a *deux ex machina* of causality. Culture's autonomy, and yours and my autonomy, are always relative to the structure of the social formation, its forces, and their balance. Culture is not *ex nihilo* autonomous, nor is it *ex individuo* autonomous, arising from individual action. Autonomy is always immanent in and relative to the social structure.

Repressive Region

There are constant threats of mission drift and outright disruption in the social formtaion, both from within a social formation and outside a social formation. Challenges come at the formation constantly. While the modes of production are how people make life with each other in a basic way, and the ideological region is where they live this life in their own idiosyncratic rhythm and reproduce relations of all kinds, the repressive region keeps things in line. The repressive region is what all subjects in the formation may have to deal with if they break the rules. The repressive region steps in when there's unrest. The repressive region holds down the fort. Rather than the idiosyncratic ensemble of ideological state apparatuses, the repressive region has laws, police, prisons, government, courts, and the military. These variations exert a kind of downward-facing force in the formation, ensuring the social formation functions through repression. These repressive state apparatuses intervene and create consequences when things go wrong, get out of hand, or someone/some group steps out of line.

> This theory not only concerns the *economic* problems of transition (forms of planning the adaptation of the forms of planning to different specific stages of the transition, according to the particular conditions of the countries considered); it also concerns the *political* problems (forms of the State, forms of the political organization of the revolutionary party, the forms and nature of the revolutionary party's intervention in the different domains of political, economic, and ideological activity) and *ideological* problems of transition (politics in the religious, moral, juridical, aesthetic and philosophical, etc., domains). (Althusser, *Philosophy and the Spontaneous Philosophy of the Scientists and Other Essays, Theory, Theoretical Practice and Theoretical Formation: Ideology and Ideological Struggle*, 1990c, p. 20)

Thanksgiving

Think of Thanksgiving dinner, a holiday for some in the United States. I'll use my own (somewhat stereotypical) experience as an example of elements, variations, forces, and regions at work.

Economic Region
There are people, machines, animals, and land that combine such that there's a turkey and all the side dishes on the table; not to mention the table itself, chairs, flatware, house, and clothing the dinner guests and hosts wear. Where did the turkey come from? How was it raised, slaughtered, sold, and bought? Who did this work and where? Economic forces, combined elements in variations and regions and levels emerging as relations of production and means

of production, caused the turkey to be on the table. Without the turkey—or whatever food the guests eat—there would be no Thanksgiving dinner, in a basic sense: the guests could hypothetically gather around the table, tell stories, and watch television, but without the food as such, what would the dinner be? There might be stories, meanings, histories, practices, rituals, and traditions. But you can't eat culture. In the last instance, if these economic variations weren't in place, there wouldn't be a Thanksgiving dinner because there would be no food. The base force bringing food to the table is the productive force.

Ideological Region

You can't eat culture, but there's no eating without culture. Thanksgiving dinner isn't just turkey in this base economic sense. You can eat turkey whenever. There are rituals, stories, and the meaning of Thanksgiving that make it what it is: that all-too-rosy picture of colonizer pilgrims eating in harmony with indigenous peoples; fall colors of red, brown, and orange; pride in the country; family gathered around. There are books, shows, songs, paintings, images, whole curricula and messages that communicate these Thanksgiving rituals, which people receive and enact and resist in idiosyncratic ways, twisting them to fit their moments and interests and circumstances. Young people learn the stories (traditional, dominant, or insurgent). Older people teach them. Apparatuses like families and schools and churches and newspapers and television and movie studios, radio stations and sports franchises and their attendant websites all reproduce these messages. Without these meanings, stories, and their variations there would be no Thanksgiving as such either. This ritual-force in the social formation promoting meanings and codes, culture, is an ideological and reproductive force in the social formation: they make sure Thanksgiving continues to mean what it means over time.

Repressive Region

All the elements and variations in the economy that brought the turkey to the table (and all the apparatuses reproducing its stories) are enforced by contracts, property law, labor law, environmental law. These laws were written by lawyers and policymakers, ratified by appointed and elected officials, and they're enforced by police of various kinds. Thanksgiving and all those that celebrate it in the social formation must be protected from harm. Those who break the laws are prosecuted and convicted and sent to prisons. If people from outside the country's borders threaten that territory, the military might be sent to stop the threat or gain ground for the social formation in its name. This force is a repressive force working in concert with the reproductive force to maintain the modes of production as Thanksgiving comes around every year.

The Three Social Forces: Productive, Reproductive, Repressive

From the point of view of the economy, a mode of production doesn't have a protective force that maintains its relations and keeps them in place. Another force is needed: this is the repressive force. Neither the economy nor government have a way of remaking themselves in continuity as its elements weaken, die and are born. They can't tell the good news about themselves, spread the word and teach their elements how to live with it and in it. This remaking and maintaining force is the reproductive ideological force. From the point of view of culture, humans and non-humans have to eat. They can't eat their culture. The culture won't fill their stomachs or heat their houses or protect their bodies from ecological forces. As they learn, create and promote their idiosyncratic meanings, they require nourishment. This nourishment is the productive force of the social formation. People set up protected boundaries around these nourishment practices and ritual practices. These boundaries and their protective practices are the repressive force of the social formation. Finally, from the point of view of repressive forces, there must be rituals and economies to protect and serve. There must be interests to defend, territory to guard and win, reasons for the violence: something to fight for.

These are three forces in a social formation, whose variations and regions and levels differ radically across contexts, peoples, territories. According to the law of uneven development, each variation expresses a force and exerts it relatively autonomously. All the forces have a role in changing the social formation. None of them express the essence of the formation. None of them act alone. They act in concert, as an ensemble. The variations exert forces and change at differential rates, which can be measured by the comminution or diminution of relations among the elements, which themselves break down or form up, weaken and strengthen. These forces have tendencies that set up limits in the formation. These limits come into tension with one another, forming faults and cracks. There are downpourings, rises, upswellings. The forces create determinant circumstances and situations in their combinations.

The Hut and the Theater

Marx used architectural language to talk about social formations: base and superstructure, or *bau* and *uberbau*. The economy is the base and the political, ideological, and cultural aspects of society are a superstructure, like in a building. The English philosopher G. A. Cohen illustrates this further by describing a hut. The hut's posts are rooted in the ground. The posts would fall over in a strong wind, however, if there were no top-down force acting on them to keep them in place. The roof is a kind of superstructure and the posts form a base. The base holds up the roof and the roof keeps the posts in place. Althusser develops this further, adding complexity to the metaphor, by likening the base and superstructure to a play in a theater. There are superstructures and a base, but what's happening in this building is a production with actors, audience, authors, and directors. Productions of plays vary each night but have a similar script, key players, a theme or tendency. There's no clear author. Things are not cut and dry: there's a performance, representation, activity, passivity, darkness and light. Putting these analogies together, the productive force is rooted in the earth, the repressive forces push down keeping the economic force in place, and the ideological force normalizes life in the structure through practices: the theater of what it means to live under that roof and on that ground.

> Lenin analyzed what constituted the characteristics of [the situation's] structure: the essential articulations, the interconnections, the strategic nodes on which the possibility and the fate of any revolutionary practice depended; the disposition and relations typical of the contradictions in a determinate country (semi-feudal and semi-colonialist, and yet imperialist) in the period in which the principal contradiction was approaching explosion. This is what is irreplaceable in Lenin's texts: the analysis of the structure of a conjuncture...the structure of his practical object: with the typicality of the contradictions, with their displacements, their condensations, and the 'fusion' in revolutionary rupture that they produced; in short, with the 'current situation' that they constituted. That is why the theory of the 'weakest link' is identical with the theory of the 'decisive link.' (Althusser, *For Marx, On the Materialist Dialectic*, 2005b, pp. 179–180)

> In pointing this out, the Marxist topography refers any questioner to his place in the historical process: *this* is the place which you occupy, and *this* is where you must move to in order to change things. Archimedes wanted only a single fixed point in order to lift up the world. The Marxist topography names the place where you must fight because that is where the fight will take place for the transformation of the world. But this place is no longer a point, nor is it fixed—it is an articulated system of positions governed by the determination of the last instance. (Althusser, *Philosophy and the Spontaneous Philosophy of the Scientists and Other Essays, Is it Simple to be a Marxist in Philosophy?*, 1990a, p. 220)

Naked Capitalism

Among news websites, I like *Naked Capitalism* the most, specifically the aggregations of hyperlinks in the morning and afternoon. The editors organize the links by section and each section is layered. Typically the environment comes first, after which is trade and politics and war, followed by culture. Business news is near the bottom, along with technology and more culture. Their approach is like a news website brought to you by the theory of social formation. It's as though the website is set up according to the theory. The ordering of these sections from top to bottom falls along the lines of the theory of social formations: repressive, ideological, and economic forces. The aggregated links are layered like sediment, dross, through which one can trace threads, pressures, effects. The immanent structure of society is studyable through *Naked Capitalism*, whereas most news networks choose to individuate stories and themes for the reader, focusing on the president for instance, or the government and war exclusively, leaving business to another segment or channel.

Home Ownership

I find memoir and field notes a powerful way to express this theory of social formations. Take home ownership. I'm privileged and secure enough to have had the chance to do this, and recently purchased a home in Philadelphia, Pennsylvania, USA. As a subject in this social formation (urban northeast coast United States of America, 2018) it wouldn't make sense to understand home ownership as anything but overdetermined by a set of repressive, reproductive, and productive forces, each one emerging from regions with their own variations of elements and relations, operating at different rates of change, all of which converged upon and within and from me, as subject, as I bought the house. I was a bearer of this social structure, both in the sense of giving birth to the social structure and shouldering that social structure as I enacted the practices of buying the house.

The process of purchasing property, coming to possess it, is legal as much as financial. The possession itself is economic and the prices and values associated with the housing market is thoroughly economic, but the legal category of property and the contracts involved in ensuring the passage of funds between buyer and seller, is all repressive. There are laws which support the system of private ownership, regulations setting interest rates, etc. The people involved in ensuring this act of consumption all have personalities, backgrounds, business models: lawyers, inspectors, real estate agents, mortgage lenders, brokers, contractors. There are practices and actions and rituals in place, which differ between circumstances. The final signing was quite a scene. As buyers, once we had negotiated the price and gone through the many viewings, contracts, and paperwork involved in settling on the price, we sat around a table at the mortgage lender's office, the seller on one side and us on the other. Several loan officers were present to walk us through the process. We made small talk and laughed. Everyone on the seller's team was Black, on the buyer's side white. Throughout the process my partner was treated differently because she is a woman. I came to see that I should be present for as many interactions as possible regarding the house, even if I said nothing, because people in this part of the economic and repressive regions treat people identifying as women less seriously than they do people who identify as men.

All these variations expressed forces which layered together along the lines of dominant relations of production, in this case the relations of housing consumption since we were purchasing the house. But as Marx wrote, consumption is productive. Prices, preferences, wealth, privileges, supply, demand, banking practices like mortgages, interest rates, and insurance all exerted economic forces while contracts and regulations, furnished by laws articulated upon and within the housing market, exerted repressive force, while all the fine-grained practices, gestures, and movements exerted ideological forces reproducing the imagined relations that make everyone in this social formation go all by themselves. We all related to one another and the world of things through the forces of the relations we enacted, ultimately reproducing the imagined relations anew by acting them out with and for one another.

It was a victorious day for privately-owned residential real estate. We lived out the predominant imagined relation to real conditions that makes subjects go all by themselves when they can afford to purchase a house in Philadelphia. We did the dance in the theater of the social formation, our social structure immanently emerging all around us in the effects of all these practices. All in attendance witnessed these requisite rituals, and it was good for the ideology and social structure whose variations and relations call for private residential ownership. We were its bearers in our actions, in our relations and interminglings with forces, each of which were relatively autonomous. The social structure reproduced immanently as we bought the house.

> It is very important to understand why Marx considers men in this case only as 'supports' of a relation, or 'bearers' of a function in the production process, determined by the production relation. It is not at all because he reduces men in their concrete life to simple bearers of functions: he considers as such in this respect because the capitalist production relation reduces them to simple function within the infrastructure, in production: that is, in exploitation. (Althusser, *Philosophy and the Spontaneous Philosophy of the Scientists and Other Essays, Is it Simple to be a Marxist in Philosophy?*, 1990a, p. 236)

> Far be it from me to denigrate this great humanist tradition, whose historical merit was to have struggled against feudalism, against the Church, and against their ideologists, and to have given man a status and dignity. But far be it from us, I think, to deny the fact that this humanist ideology, which produced great works and great thinkers, is inseparably linked to the rising bourgeoisie whose aspirations it expressed, translating and transporting the demands of a commercial and capitalist economy sanctioned by a new system of law, the old Roman law revised as bourgeois commercial law. Man as free subject, free man as a subject of his actions and his thoughts, is first of all man free to possess and to buy, the subject of law. (Althusser, *Philosophy and the Spontaneous Philosophy of the Scientists and Other Essays, Is it Simple to be a Marxist in Philosophy?*, 1990a, p. 233)

Freedom

If we live in a structure where relations and forces create pressure, and we are elements in these relations—if we are bearers of structure—is there room for freedom?

I've given two responses to this question so far. First, in several sections above, I've argued that freedom is a quality of the social structure and not individuals. Because society is a social formation and social structure is immanent in its effects, freedom is immanent in the relative autonomy of practices in their formation. Elements form into variations which form into other variations, all of which express forces as they interact with one another. Determination, or how actions and events and people determine their fates, are relative to the indexes of effectivity in their social formations. They have freedom to swerve, freedom to maneuver, but that freedom is always relatively dependent on the balance of forces they exist within. Freedom is a feature of the structure. Humans like you or me, the groups we're part of, are bearers of this social structure in a dual sense: first in the sense of birth, because we give birth to the social structure when we enact practices in the formation and second in the sense of shouldering, because we inherit the social structure. We cannot control the society into which we're born, but there's always a contingency to the formation of the society. Things could always shift. They could always be otherwise. And the practices we enact, the imagined relations we misunderstand, shirk, or take up and take on in the conjuncture, can always shift the balance of forces. We have that freedom, not because of some *ex nihilo* feature of our species or its cultural practices, but rather because the real object of society is uneven.

But there's a second response to the freedom question. Dislocation and unevenness can be applied to any part of the real object, any item in the world of things, including beings like you or me. The theory of relative autonomy says that forces and their variations and elements and relations can shift idiosyncratically and the reasons for this shift are always exceptional, specific to those overdetermined circumstances. Elements in their relations can move, settle and swerve in unique ways relative to their circumstances. Like rock formations set solidly, the grains and forces running through them are always moving, sometimes imperceptibly. No matter how solid-feeling or stable-seeming, the variations in a formation exist in a space of contingency. There's freedom in this concept of structure because the structure is an absent cause, like Voltron: any given change is the result of multiple complex forces acting on a balance of forces. Things shift and are always shifting and will always shift. There's freedom in this shifting. The same goes for ourselves. Like the layers of the bolus in the interpellation machine from the first chapter, each individual—as a subject in social structure—is a formation of elements in relation to one another. Each of us is a set of structured variations living within a larger set of structured variations. Individual freedom is the awareness of one's own unevenness.

Althusser was anti-humanist, but this anti-humanism comes from a commitment to anti-essentialism. To say that I am essentially a human being with certain characteristics is to ignore the law of dislocation. But words have concepts behind them, and the word freedom need not have an essentialist concept behind it. Freedom could have a materialist concept. Materialist freedom derives from the relative autonomy of variations in a structure, both the social structure and the individual's structured variations within that structure.

An Allegory for Social Structure

Two people live in a building. They were born there to parents who were also born there. One person lives in the basement, underground, and the other lives on the second floor—two floors up. It's dark and musty in the basement, there are few windows and scarce light. The second floor in contrast is airy and bright—it has a view with trees outside.

To get and maintain their basic resources (food, shelter, clothing, education, transportation, healthcare, leisure time, etc) each person has to go to the first floor and play a game. The game is sometimes a sitting down game, like chess, sometimes more physical, like a race. The winner of the game gets a higher rate of resources than the loser: more food, better education, faster healthcare, available transportation, more leisure.

Every morning the upstairs person takes an escalator down to the first floor to play the day's game. The escalator doesn't go to the basement, so the downstairs person walks up a set of stairs every morning and evening after playing the game of the day.

Since before either players can remember, for their parents and grandparents and great grandparents and most likely before that, their daily lives in this building unfold the same way. Each game they play has a set of rules, but no matter the outcome—whether the downstairs person plays harder or better than the upstairs person—the upstairs person is declared winner of the game. The upstairs person always wins just by virtue of living upstairs. Even if the downstairs player technically wins the game, follows all the rules and beats the upstairs person, the downstairs person is declared loser just by virtue of living downstairs. According to the leaders of the building and common wisdom passed down from their parents, that's just "human nature." Upstairs people win. Downstairs people lose.

Everyday the downstairs person walks up the stairs, which are steep and rickety but not impossible to climb, and the upstairs person comes down the escalator. They have families to provide for, friends they spend time with, lives they lead—and they each have cultures shaped by the winning and losing over time. The downstairs people and upstairs people each have their own distinctive art, dialects, philosophies, histories, and attitudes about each other, the building itself, and its other occupants. Certainly each have their own joys and sufferings, frustrations and difficulties. Certainly they share physiological similarities and can understand one another's language (most of the time). But they live from birth to death on fundamentally different floors, one lower than the other, and this shapes much of their experience.

One day, on their way to the first floor for their daily game, something feels different. The air is fresher downstairs, staler upstairs. The escalator breaks and fresh air streams to the basement somehow. They'd both heard and felt construction going on in the building the previous night, which is infrequent but happens sometimes. The previous night there had been some kind of pounding and knocking, and yelling between what sounded like warring factions, like a battle, but it was too faint to make out exactly what was being said.

The two sit down and play their game, unnerved.

Something strange happens. The downstairs person wins the game and is declared winner.

They are both shocked, but in different ways. The upstairs person, from a culture of winning, has never experienced this kind of loss before. They still have their winnings from generations of victory, yet the feeling of losing is upsetting to them. They are very angry. This is not how it's supposed to go. It's just human nature for them to win. Their culture is built on the premise of success, action, and work and it tells them through its art and history that they deserve to win—and that the downstairs people are the ones that deserve to lose. They have come to feel that they deserve their success—after all, they are always declared winners of all the games. But now they've lost. They feel frustrated and threatened.

The downstairs person on the other hand is flooded with a sense of possibility and happy confusion—they can win?, they ask themselves. It wasn't really an option before. It was human nature for them to lose. Their culture has been built around the trauma of fruitless work, ongoing loss, and resignation. And now they have extra resources. What will they do with them? Could they win again?

Looking across the table from one another, the upstairs person—who rarely speaks to the downstairs person—says:

"I can't believe I lost, this is all wrong."

The downstairs person, who has focused so much tense energy on the upstairs person for so long, responds with graceful anger:

"You have no idea what it means to lose."

In the Last Instance: Theory of Movable Types

There's disagreement and controversy over which force—productive, reproductive, repressive, ecological—is the most important and impactful in a social formation. Which force should we focus on when trying to change the social formation, which admixture of priorities we should have in strategy? Some say the repressive (electoral politics, policy), others says ideological (cultural practices), still others say the ecological (environmentalism). Marxists tend to think that the productive force, or the economy, is the place to focus on. Althusser agreed, but in a distinct way.

Althusser used the phrase "in the last instance" to talk about how the economic force is determinate, effective, and causal (the phrase is Friedrich Engels'.) A tension emerges here in readings of Marx. Some say that to be a Marxist means to think of the economy as a bottom-line force, to which the repressive and ideological forces ultimately respond. They say that cultural and political practices are a function of the economy, or reduce those practices to class struggle. But Althusser's concept of the base as being determinate in the last instance is different. First, to say that cultural or economic practices are "a function of" the base is to make an essentializing claim and Althusser is against this across the board, as we know. Second, making this essentializing claim would go against the law of uneven development, specifically relative autonomy. If cultural practices and politics were a function of the economy they wouldn't have any autonomy whatsoever.

Rather, while Althusser says that the economic force is determinant in the last instance, he also says that this final moment never arrives. There are only regions and levels of the structure; structured variations in the real object moving relatively autonomously at differential rates with this differential indexes of effectivity. Any change in the real object comes about from a set of forces, in overdetermination or underdetermination, which shifts that balance. This uneven stance about the economy's efficacy means the set of forces will necessarily include a combination of at least two of the different kinds of forces. And since there's always a balance of forces, societies (as social formations) have particular determinant circumstances that require specific interventions to shift their composition.

This last position about particular circumstances shows that Althusser's is a theory of movable types: Althusser's theory—with its commitments to dislocation and uneven development—lends itself to an analysis of social formations using different, idiosyncratic articulations of concepts. In some social formations, religion exerts such a outsized reproductive force that an intervention in that social formation requires inordinate emphasis on the ideological region. In other social formations, there are weak repressive regions, or the economic force is heavily regulated. Because social forces are relatively autonomous, you have to consider how to move the concepts in the theory around to match the idiosyncrasy of the terrain you want to shift.

But calling this kind of movable types analysis "idiosyncratic" is inaccurate. To be idiosyncratic means being unique or different or exceptional. Uniqueness and difference and exceptionality imply that there is a normal, ideal, non-unique, run-of-the-mill balance of forces. But the theory of social formations rejects any such normal balance. Every balance is unique, every formation has a set of exceptional circumstances. Every moment in every region is exceptional. Without exception, each situation is exceptional.

According to the law of dislocation, no object of knowledge—no concept, not even Marxist philosophy itself—will ever be located in the real object of the social formation, but rather ideas about the social information are part of the social formation in their own level, competing in their own balance where a set of concepts will dominate. Philosophy, concepts, and ideas (like this one here, behind the words I write) are part of the ideological reproductive force. Claiming that any force is always the most impactful, the one to look at, the bottom-line, wouldn't follow this law. So Althusser would never claim this, which is consistent with the theory he produced.

The theory of social formations, according to the laws of dislocation and uneven development, is a theory of movable types: activists and scholars should articulate these types depending on the state of the formation, the elements in their variations and regions and levels, the forces in ascendency and diminution. They should combine the elements of the theory into variations that increase the likelihood of naming and creating shifts in the balance of forces.

Academic and intellectual controversy aside, what matters is strategy: where to push in the balance of forces, and when and how to push so there's a shift. The key is whether a group can make gains given the circumstances, can marshall the right forces in the right way to make the right kind of torsion or explosion or swelling, and navigate the terrain so their social relations become dominant in their structure. Lenin called this finding "the weak link in the chain." If you can break this link the whole chain falls off. If you move the right grain, squeeze the right region, track the sequence of pressures and tensions and potential torsions (that is, if you're scientific and experimental), you have a shot at finding that place in the structure that could create the upswell or downgrade needed to defeat dominant forces.

The theory of movable types is like a framework-toolbox to help keep us ontologically honest when figuring out the balance of forces, mapping the terrain, and plotting interventions that alter the very relations that constitute its structure. The bottom line isn't knowledge of any natural law, nor mastery of nature, but rather to shift the forces. The theory compels us to be realistic, stay open, remember that there are no guarantees and look exactly for the place to add force, where to block it, and how to decide what requires exogenous or endogenous energy. At its best, the theory keeps us open to the contingency of social stuff as we fight, because at the heart of the theory of movable types is the idea that every thing is a mess, society is a social formation with a specific terrain, a balance of particular forces where some variations dominate, but never forever. The theory of movable types prevents us from fixing types in place, settling or reifying or idealizing anything too much. Treating society as a social formation, the social as an immanent real object, should compel us, by virtue of the theory itself, to attend to the elements and their relations and the variations and regions of variations in our contexts, to figure out the truth: what to say, what to think, and what to do to shift those variations. We can be right or wrong; we must do tests and experiments; we should try to make predictions. Ideology gets in the way here to some degree, and science is what we have to do to get that truth—but this concept of ideology, science, and truth is somewhat different than what we're used to.

> In the determination of the topography, the last *instance* really is the *last* instance. If it is *the last one*, as in the legal image which it invokes (court of the last instance), that is because there are *others*, those which figure in the legal-political and ideological superstructure. The mention of the last instance in determination thus plays a double role: it divides Marx sharply off from all mechanistic explanations, and opens up within determination the functioning of different instances, the functioning of a real difference in which the dialectic is inscribed. The topography thus signifies that the determination in the last instance by the economic base can be grasped only within a differentiated, therefore complex and articulated whole (the '*Gliderung*'), in which the determination in the last instance fixes the real difference of other instances, relative autonomy and their own mode of reacting on the base itself. (Althusser, *Philosophy and the Spontaneous Philosophy of the Scientists and Other Essays, Is it Simple to be a Marxist in Philosophy?*, 1990a, p. 215)

> In order to really understand what one 'reads' and studies in these theoretical, political and historical works, one must directly experience oneself that two realities determine them through and through: the reality of theoretical practice (science, philosophy) in its concrete life; the reality of the practice of revolutionary class struggle in its concrete life, in close contact with the masses. For if theory enables us to understand the laws of history, it is not intellectuals, nor even theoreticians, it is the masses who make history. It is essential to learn with theory—but at the same time and crucially, it is essential to learn with the masses. (Althusser, *Lenin and Philosophy and Other Essays, Philosophy as a Revolutionary Weapon*, 1971, p. 20)

CHAPTER 5

Conclusion: Ideology, Truth, Science

> When a stick is bent in the wrong direction, said Lenin, it is necessary, if you want to put matters right—that is, if you want to straighten it and keep it straight—to grasp it and bend it durably in the opposite direction. This simple formula seems to me to contain a whole theory of the effectiveness of speaking the truth, a theory deeply rooted in Marxist practice. Contrary to the whole rationalist tradition, which requires only a straight, true idea in order to correct a bent, false idea, Marxism considers that ideas have a historical existence only insofar as they are taken up and incorporated by the materialism of social relations. Behind the relations between simple ideas there thus stand relations of force, which place certain ideas in power (those which can schematically called the ruling ideology) and hold other ideas in submission (which can be called the oppressed ideology), until the relation of force is changed. It follows that if you want to change historically existing ideas, even in the apparently abstract domain called philosophy, you cannot content yourself with simply preaching the naked truth, and waiting for its anatomical obviousness to 'enlighten' minds, as our 18th century ancestors used to say: you are forced, since you want to force a change in ideas, to recognize the force which is keeping them bent, by applying a counterforce capable of destroying this power and bending the stick in the opposite direction so as to put the ideas right.
>
> Louis Althusser, *Philosophy and the Spontaneous Philosophy of the Scientists and Other Essays: Is it Simple to be a Marxist in Philosophy?*, 1990a, p. 210

∴

Ambivalence

Althusser is known as a theorist of ideology and he's known for drawing attention to ideology in a path-breaking and unique way. He worked out a concept of ideology defining it as an individual's imagined relationship to their real conditions of existence. Ideology, as a relation, is a practice that works through allusion and illusion and propagates via interpellations in ideological state apparatuses. The way that Althusser writes the word ideology in his books and essays is more varied than his own theory of it, however, which he did not work out until later in his career. The texts he's best known for cast the word in an ambivalent way.

The ambivalence is between what Jan Rehmann and others call ideology theory and ideology critique. Ideology theory says ideology is inescapable: everyone has an ideology, every position or thought is ideological, and the social-political world is a complex mixture of ideologies competing, dying, and being born. Ideology critique however says ideology is a negative thing, an obfuscating veil which confounds others into believing false things. In an ideology critique, ideology is escapable—you just have to wake up to the truth. Ideology critique says that ideology is an enemy to truth. In this case ideology is escapable and should be escaped, either through righteousness or some privileged method which gives you access to the truth.

Althusser sometimes uses an ideology theory, other times ideology critique. The law of dislocation doesn't have a clear position on this. Because the real object is never the object of knowledge and vice versa, theories are always parallel with the world of things. At first, this seems like just another ideology theory. Since thought and the world don't converge, there's only ever ideology and nothing is true or false. It may seem, in other words, like the law of dislocation is relativistic. But claiming that the law of dislocation implies such a relativist ideology theory presumes that truth and falsity are only ever established by the convergence of thought with reality. This convergence theory is one theory of truth, but it isn't the only one. There might be a theory of truth that follows the law of dislocation, with a different concept, one that doesn't rely on thought converging with reality for there to be truth. To phrase it as a question: what would it be like to do science and follow the law of dislocation?

In Althusser's writings, this issue is never fully decided. There are times when Althusser claims that expressivists and empiricists can only have ideological concepts that are contaminated with distorted ideas. Their heads are full of ideology, he sometimes says, acting like toxins to be expunged or diseases to be healed. The medicine or purifier in this case would be science, a theory of theoretical practice that finds openings at the closures of essentialist circles of knowledge and thereby accesses the truth. There are other times when Althusser is repentant for implying the above, however. He apologizes in *Essays in Self-Criticism* for coming across as positivist, theoreticist, and getting within a hand's breadth of empiricism himself. Still other times, he's clear that that all concepts are ideological because they're always at some point in the knowledge production process (whether common sense, methodological, or newly hammered out concepts). Finally, there are still other places where he claims outright that we never escape ideology, that any concept is ideological since any set of ideas are imagined relationships to an ultimately complex and variable set of real conditions.

Althusser is always trying to articulate what's special about Karl Marx's writing and philosophy, but for the purpose of advancing the cause of socialism and communism. To the extent that he reads other scholars and activists making claims about Marx, and finds problematics and concepts and concretes-in-thought that make claims to being the Marxist object of knowledge (but don't meet his criterion for what the Marxist object of knowledge is) he becomes spiky and writes with an ideology critique. Admittedly, this is because he believes there's a "true" account of Marxist philosophy. Yet Althusser's theory of ideology, as we saw, is an ideology theory that would never permit such a thing as a "true" account of anything that isn't to some degree ideological.

How could one of the best theorists of ideology, whose theory of ideology is an ideology theory, help himself to ideology critique like this? What's his theory of truth, in other words?

Truth as Correctness

I propose a solution which draws from the French philosopher of language Jean-Jacques Lecercle. The law of dislocation implies neither an ideology theory nor an ideology critique. What it means to say something is true, stipulate a concept of reality, and hammer out how our knowledge relates to reality is distinctive in Althusser's (which, he would say, is just Marx's) theory. Saying that the law of dislocation implies an ideology theory, for example, projects a concept of truth onto the theory (probably an empiricist concept). Empiricists would say that ideology theory is relativistic, that according to such a theory ideology is inescapable and that therefore there is no truth or falsity. But this is specious, since it only makes sense if the convergence of thought with reality—a rejection of the law of dislocation—is the only theory of truth. But it isn't, especially for Marxists.

In other words, just because ideology is inescapable doesn't mean that there's no truth and falsity. It's clear both from Althusser's own writing and the communist tradition he belonged to that what it means for something to be true isn't the same as what it means for an empirical or expressive account to be true. Lecercle has argued that Althusser's theory of truth, inspired as it is by Lenin and Gramsci, is one of correctness. A statement is true if it correctly names the conjuncture so that the balance of forces shift, hopefully (but not necessarily) against the hegemony of oppressive and exploitative social relations. If a phrase or word, and the concepts behind them, are part of the compulsion of elements in regions of the social structure to resolve a tension, begin a torsion, or ignite an explosion or sliding or swelling at the site of the structure's instabilities, then we know the statement is correct. This theory of truth is an activist theory of truth. It doesn't require a convergence with reality, yet there is feedback from reality about whether the thoughts and propositions are correct about the world of things.

According to this activist theory of truth, there is an ideology theory where statements are true and false. There can also be non-imaginary relations to real conditions: in a word, science. But this science isn't necessarily the science of lab coats and test tubes and natural laws. This science is a sweet science of maneuver, like boxing. This sweet science is the science of finding what spot to hit, how hard, and when to do so in order to defeat your opponent in the struggle for victory. Lenin said that for a revolution you have to find the weakest link in the chain of the social structure and break it. The concepts and statements that lead to such a break of the weakest link are correct and, according to the concept of truth as correctness, true. Doing science means not accepting the first set of concepts that come your way, but to sift, plan, watch, and see what you have to think to defeat opponents, shift the balance of forces, generate practices that exert the right kind of force at the right time to force a rupture. This sweet science requires inquiry, experimentation through action, and evaluation. There's a reality "out there," sure, and you can be wrong about it. Just not in the way the normal scientists think. Philosophy in this theory draws lines of demarcation between the positions themselves, whereas science builds out the territory. Typically, the border lines come after the exploration: science leads the way and philosophy follows.

> The history of philosophy 'proceeds' very differently: via a *struggle for domination* by the new philosophical forms against those that were once dominant. The history of philosophy is a struggle between tendencies realized in philosophical formations, and it is always a struggle for domination. But the paradox is that this struggle results only in the replacement of one domination by another, and not in the pure and simple elimination of a past formation (as 'error': for there is no error in philosophy, in the sense that there is in the sciences)—that is, of the adversary. The adversary is never totally defeated and *therefore never totally suppressed*, totally *erased from historical existence*. It is only *dominated* and it lives on under the domination of the new philosophical formation that has overcome it after a very protracted battle: it lives on as a *dominated* philosophical formation, and is naturally ready to re-emerge whenever the conjuncture gives the signal and furnishes occasion...

> It is not a question of simply *enumerating* philosophies, asking why they exist or subsist alongside one another, but rather of examining the philosophical formations which, old as they may be, still exist today in subordinate but still living forms, *dominated* by other formations, which have conquered in struggle, or are in the process of conquering, something that must be called 'power.' (Althusser, *Philosophy and the Spontaneous Philosophy of the Scientists and Other Essays, Philosophy and the Spontaneous Philosophy of the Scientists*, 1990b, p. 122)

Gold

Certainly the gold is part of the dross in Althusser's theory of truth as correctness, but only because humans value gold and search for gold to enrich themselves. Yet there should still be a way to subscribe to the law of dislocation and admit that gold is worth more than salt under certain circumstances, or dirt, or any other sediment it may be mixed with. It's easy to do this in the analogy of gold and dross, because gold is valuable in most economies. That's why humans extract it. The fact that it's valuable, that having a lot of it makes a difference in the balance of forces, means that gold doesn't have the same value as other substances. Its value is why humans pan for it, and that fact makes it what it is. There's a complex and structured set of variations in reality. There's a social formation that values gold. There's an ideology that values gold. There are people with that ideology that look for and find gold. So it goes with ideology, truth, and science. Thought never converges with reality, yet certain thoughts, when people have them in their heads, make a difference—or are the residue of differences made—in the balance of forces. These statements are true because they correctly name the balance of forces and are part of a compulsion that shifts those forces.

This theory isn't relativist: truth doesn't depend on position. Truth rather depends on your position in the existing balance of forces, which you don't choose, and the extent to which you're part of a force shifting the balance. You can be wrong about what will shift the balance of forces (the election of Donald Trump, and the Democratic Party's lack of anticipation of this result being one example). Yet Althusser's theory of truth as correctness isn't idealist, since truths are not references to simple internal essences, natural laws, or Ideas. The truths aren't there in reality, just like gold isn't there in dross unless someone is panning it and makes a difference in the balances of forces.

> Generality I, for example, the concept of 'fruit' is not the product of an 'operation of abstraction' performed by a 'subject' (consciousness, or even that mythological subject 'practice')—but the result of a complex process of elaboration which involves several distinct concrete practices on different levels, empirical, technical, and ideological. (To return to our rudimentary example, the concept of fruit is itself the product of distinct practices, dietary, agricultural, even magical, religious and ideological practices—in its own origins.) So long as knowledge has not broken with ideology, every Generality I will be deeply impregnated by ideology, which is one of the basic practices essential to the existence of the social whole. The act of abstraction whereby the pure essence is extracted from concrete individuals is an ideological myth. In essence, Generality I is inadequate to the essence of the objects from which abstraction should extract it. It is this inadequacy that theoretical practice reveals and removes by the transformation of Generality I into Generality III [via Generality II]. (Althusser, *For Marx, On the Materialist Dialectic*, 2005b, p. 191)

Science as Sweet Science

Pierce Egan, who wrote some of the first comprehensive histories of the sport of boxing, called boxing a "sweet science." In Althusser's theory, science is a sweet science of struggle, position, and maneuver. Althusser's opponent, throughout his career, was misunderstood Marxism. This adversary led, he believed, to failed communist projects from 1939 to 1956 and beyond. His science was a sweet science of defeating opponents in the region of concepts, received ideologies that hadn't been worked on well and led to bad outcomes in the larger struggle to defeat one of the most powerful tensions in the modern balance of forces: exploitation of workers. Althusser saw misunderstandings, incorrect thinking, and went out to correct them. He took a Generality I about Marxism, used a Generality II developed through Marxism to produce a new Generality III about Marxism. This meant he had commitments to a true Marxism, but not in the transcendental sense of his thought converging with a reality of the One True Marxism, but rather in the immanent sense of his thought being correct about Marxism so that Marxists could think clearly about building socialism and communism. He went about examining concepts to get to the correct ones and vindicate strategies for making socialism that would not disappoint him and his comrades. Althusser succeeded partly in doing this,

CONCLUSION: IDEOLOGY, TRUTH, SCIENCE

at least in the history of philosophy: his thinking shifted the balance of forces in the intellectual region of the social formation. His theory made an impact on how people think about Marxism. Whether that theory ultimately helps to shift the balance of forces in the larger social formation is up to those of us reading, thinking, learning, teaching, and fighting.

> There is no teaching of pure knowledge that is not at the same time a *savoir-faire*—that is, the definition of a know-how-to-act-in-relation-to-this-knowledge, and to its *theoretical and social function*. (Althusser, *Philosophy and the Spontaneous Philosophy of the Scientists and Other Essays, Philosophy and the Spontaneous Philosophy of the Scientists*, 1990b, p. 94)

> For intellectuals, nothing could be more difficult than perceiving the ideology conveyed by education, and by its curriculum, its forms and its practices. (Althusser, *Philosophy and the Spontaneous Philosophy of the Scientists and Other Essays, Philosophy and the Spontaneous Philosophy of the Scientists*, 1990b, p. 95)

Afterword: Studying the Dross

Tyson E. Lewis

Althusser always had pedagogical concerns. He criticized Marx for making his text *Capital: Volume One* inaccessible to the masses, and Althusser outlined an alternative way to read the book, switching around the various parts in order to foreground the theme of struggle over and against the theological analysis of the commodity and its fetishism.

Later in life, Althusser wrote several books aimed at teaching Marxism to a wide audience including *On the Reproduction of Capitalism* (1969) and *Philosophy for Non-Philosophers* (1978–1980). In the latter, he took philosophy teachers to task for isolating themselves in ivory towers, arguing that philosophy needs to connect itself back to material practices, struggles, and in the process, learn to listen to people. Other essays such as "Philosophy and the Spontaneous Philosophy of the Scientists" (1967) illustrate how everyone, to some degree, is a philosopher. The question is therefore not who is and isn't a philosopher so much as *what kind* of philosopher a person is (materialist or idealist). In short, Althusser was consistently concerned with how to teach Marxism, and experimented with various ways to teach materialism so that these ideas could have the power to influence the conjuncture of forces at work within a social formation. But these educational moves were not very successful by Althusser's standards, and he did not publish either *On the Reproduction of Capitalism* or *Philosophy for Non-Philosophers*. It would seem then that he offered no solution to an educational problematic which he adequately diagnosed.

Here we find Backer's unique contribution. Perhaps no one else has picked up on Althusser's educational problematic as Backer has in this short, powerful, and imaginative text. Indeed, this text could very well be read as an attempt to "solve" Althusser's interminable problem: how to teach his own theory to non-philosophers. In light of this thesis, I want to focus on the formal qualities of Backer's writing in order to argue that the book is pedagogical in and through its literary experimentation. Instead of positing yet another devastating critique of capitalism from the left—do we really need more convincing that capitalism is bad?—he offers a new style of writing, one that has unique educational potentials.

Certainly Althusser's writing has its own formal qualities. In particular, I would like to highlight his distinctive use of *italicization*. In his later days, Althusser wrote of the importance of the swerve in materialist philosophy. By swerving, atoms collide in unpredictable ways to produce a world. Perhaps italicizing something is the formal equivalent of the swerve, shifting a word ever so slightly so as to highlight it, bring out its meaning, curve the reader's eye toward a nuanced inflection. Such a gesture is both formal and philosophical but also *pedagogical* (notice my italicized swerve here). It is about attentiveness to *this* word and not that word. It is like the gesture of the teacher pointing something out. On this formal level, his writing experiments with solving the pedagogical issue (attentiveness) through the presentation of a philosophical argument.

Althusser was also interested in the cut. Philosophically, he made cuts within Marxism, drawing a firm demarcation line between the early and late Marx (an epistemological break, as Althusser would have it). He made cuts within philosophy between idealism and materialism. In this sense, philosophy is a weapon that draws a firm line in the sand, allowing one to take sides. And we see cuts in his work: sharp, terse prose that hacks away at dialectical influences, idealist ideology, and so on. He cuts out content, he cuts out oppositions. These cuts are not like Foucault's cuts—the careful incisions of a surgeon—so much as the cuts of a hacksaw chopping away (sometimes brutally if not crudely). Perhaps there is a brutalism here--maybe a necessary one in the messy, bloodied war for socialism. But there is also something educational about these cuts. They teach an important lesson: that philosophy is about taking sides in a struggle, that is it never a neutral practice, that it is antagonistic.

Philosophically, Althusser is somewhere between the negation of the cut (a strange reworking of Hegelianism) and the swerve (which clearly echoes Spinoza). So too, these seem to reside side-by-side in the formal dimensions of his writing as if his unconscious philosophical influences are not somewhere deep inside the content of his words so much as resting on the surface of his formulations, in plain sight. As Althusser might say, the swerve and the cut *express* his philosophical system. For this reason, it might be apt to say that in the formal qualities of the writing—the structural qualities that glue his sentences together (just as much as they rip them apart)—we find a uniquely Althusserian pedagogy: an attempt to teach philosophy as a practice of cuts and swerves.

So what is Backer's formal style? How does it teach? He clearly tells us up front: analogies, laws, and passages define the structure of the text. Analogies with media culture, imaginative images (huts, interpellation machines, beaches), and personal experiences (stories from childhood, stories of falling in love, stories from schools), the formalization of laws (the law of dislocation and the law of uneven development), and the occasional interruption of passages written by Althusser all work together to form a certain kind of pedagogical style. This is a pedagogy that is *pure dross*. It does not give us the golden nuggets of Althusser's theory, rather it entangles us in Althusser through personal, theoretical, and political strata that weave together. Everyday events from childhood come in contact with theoretical concepts, and theoretical concepts collide with political events. The text overflows with dross. Perhaps we might say that the lesson of the text is that Althusser himself is nothing but the dross of Marxist philosophy. But this is no reason why we should throw him away. If Backer is right, then we still have much to study in the dross *precisely because* it is the dross. Backer does not cut out the dross (even the bibliographic dross) nor does he swerve it per se. Instead, he invents his own pedagogical stylistics through carefully constructed analogies, the formalization of laws, and selected passages, all of which interact to form a theory-in-practice mapping of the uneven, complex, and overdetermined terrain of our lives. The voice Backer intones is not that of the expert philosopher or the aggressive ideologue, but rather of a teacher searching for creative ways to play with ideas, communicate across differences, and yet, all the while, remain militantly dedicated to a political and economic project. This is a radical shift from Althusser's difficult writing—a shift grounded in the life of an educational philosopher who has spent quality time in classrooms with students and is not afraid of the dross as a *pedagogical asset*.

Here I will conclude with a question concerning the kind of practice which education is. For Althusser, a productive practice has certain features: there is a raw material which is transformed through a certain type of work using specific instruments. In his book *Philosophy for Non-Philosophers*, Althusser discusses many types of practice, including scientific, aesthetic, political, and educational. An educational productive practice is subsumed within ideological practice. It's raw materials are are human subjects with their ideological ideas, the work is performed by Ideological State Apparatuses (ISAs), and the instruments are the instruments of teaching and learning (pedagogy, curriculum, disciplinary practices, and so on). Thus education is a struggle over ideas. isas attempt to win the consent of students (even working class students) to certain humanistic, idealist ideologies. It would seem that Althusser successfully theorized the educational practice of the ISAs but never was able to enact a materialist pedagogical alternative. Backer's insistence on counter-interpellation is important here as it opens a space and time for another kind of education to emerge, one that is antagonistic to the work of the ISAs. If Althusser once argued that philosophy follows science—that there is a lag time between the two—then perhaps we can argue that pedagogy always follows philosophy. And if this is accurate, then what is needed now more than ever is not further elaboration of Althusser's philosophy but rather his pedagogy as the "weakest link" in the materialist chain leading from theory to practice. And this is precisely why Backer's book is now more urgent than ever.

References

Althusser, L. (1971). *Lenin and philosophy and other essays*. New York, NY: Monthly Review Press.

Althusser, L. (1990a). *Philosophy and the spontaneous philosophy of the scientists and other essays: Is it simple to be a Marxist in philosophy?* London: Verso.

Althusser, L. (1990b). *Philosophy and the spontaneous philosophy of the scientists and other essays: Philosophy and the spontaneous philosophy of the scientists*. London: Verso.

Althusser, L. (1990c). *Philosophy and the spontaneous philosophy of the scientists and other essays: Theory, theoretical practice and theoretical formation: Ideology and ideological struggle*. London: Verso.

Althusser, L. (2005a). *For Marx: Contradiction and over determination*. London: Verso.

Althusser, L. (2005b). *For Marx: On the materialist dialectic*. London: Verso.

Althusser, L. (2005c). *For Marx: On the young Marx*. London: Verso.

Althusser, L. (2005d). *For Marx: The 'Piccolo Teatro': Bertolazzi and Brecht: Notes on a materialist theatre*. London: Verso.

Althusser, L. (2006). *Philosophy of the encounter: Later writings, 1978–1987*. London: Verso.

Althusser, L. (2014). *On the reproduction of capitalism: On ideology*. London: Verso.

Althusser, L., Balibar, É., Establet, R., Macherey, P., & Rancière, J. (2016). *Reading capital: The complete edition*. London: Verso.

Althusser, L. (2017). *Philosophy for non-philosophers*. London: Bloomsbury.

Index

Note: One of Althusser's most comprehensive English translators, Ben Brewster, compiled a "Glossary" of key terms in Althusserian theory in 1969. This Glossary appeared at the end of the first English translation of Reading Capital (2016) and was reissued with the full publication of that book. The following index is based on the terms in that glossary, with a few additions.

Abstract   xii, xiv, 20, 26, 29, 30, 71
Apparatus   xvii, 9, 16, 18, 19, 54–59, 72, 80

Balance of forces   xvi, 15, 16, 38, 40–45, 50–52, 64, 65, 68, 69, 73–77
Base   16–18, 56, 59–61, 68, 70
Bearer   10, 62–65

Causality   29, 57
Combination   14, 17, 41–43, 48–50, 60, 68
Concrete-in-thought, real-concrete   20–25, 28, 32
Conjuncture   41, 61, 65, 73, 74, 78
Contradiction   30, 38, 47, 52, 53, 57, 61

Dislocation   xii, 20–36, 38, 39, 50–54, 65, 68, 69, 72, 73, 75, 79

Ecologies   54
Effectivity   42, 43, 46, 64, 68
Empiricism   20, 26–28, 33, 34, 36, 72
Epistemological break   34–36, 79
Expressivism   32–34, 36

Force   xiii, xiv, xvi, 3, 8, 15–19, 25, 36, 38–46, 48, 50–65, 67–69, 71, 73–78

Generality (I–III)   23, 51, 76

Humanism   33, 65

Ideology   xii, xiv, xvii, 1, 4, 9–16, 34, 35, 44, 51, 56, 58, 63, 64, 70–77, 79
Immanent   10, 30, 49, 50, 52, 54, 57, 62, 64, 70, 76

Overdetermination   43, 47, 68

Philosophy   xii–xvii, 19, 20, 23, 25, 29, 31, 35, 37, 39, 44, 58, 61, 64, 69–71, 73–75, 77–80
Practice   1, 9, 10, 24, 26, 28, 31, 33, 36, 37, 51, 55, 56, 58–65, 67, 68, 70–72, 74, 76–80
   theoretical   24, 26, 28, 33, 58, 70, 72, 76
Problematic   xvi, 23, 34–36, 78
   geological   53
Production
   knowledge   29, 51, 72
   mode of   43, 55, 60
Productive forces   44, 59–62, 67

Relations of production   xii, 16, 17, 19, 41, 44, 53, 55, 56, 58, 63
Repression   xii, xiii, 54, 55, 58
Reproduction   xii, xvii, 9, 11, 12, 16, 17, 19, 41, 54, 55, 78

Social formation   xii, 15, 16, 18, 19, 38, 41–43, 45, 46, 52–70, 75, 77, 78
Structure   10, 11, 13–18, 25, 26, 38, 39, 43, 44, 46–52, 54–57, 60–65, 68–70, 73, 74, 79
   in dominance   39, 46, 47, 50–52, 56
Superstructure   16, 44, 60, 61, 70

Time   xii, xiii, xv, 1–8, 10, 15, 16, 19, 21, 25, 29, 30, 33, 35, 36, 38, 41, 43–46, 48, 51, 55, 56, 59, 66, 70, 72, 74, 77, 80
Totality   23, 39, 49, 50
Transcendent   49–51
Truth   24, 26, 29, 32, 35, 70–75

Uneven development   xii, 36–53, 55, 60, 68, 69, 79

Variation   16, 19, 25, 38, 39, 41–46, 50, 52, 54–60, 62–65, 68–70, 75